THE BOOK OF
RULES

THE RIGHT WAY TO DO EVERYTHING

JOSHUA BELTER

HOW
BOOKS
Cincinnati, Ohio
www.howdesign.com

For more excellent books and resources for designers, visit www.howdesign.com.

16   15   14   13   12   5 4 3 2 1

ISBN: 978-1-4403-1031-7

Distributed in Canada by Fraser Direct
100 Armstrong Avenue
Georgetown, Ontario, Canada L7G 5S4
Tel: (905) 877-4411

Distributed in the U.K. and Europe by F&W Media International, LTD
Brunel House, Forde Close, Newton Abbot, TQ12 4PU, UK
Tel: (+44) 1626 323200, Fax: (+44) 1626 323319
Email: enquiries@fwmedia.com

Distributed in Australia by Capricorn Link
P.O. Box 704, Windsor, NSW 2756 Australia
Tel: (02) 4577-3555

Edited by Amy Owen
Designed by Grace Ring
Illustrated by Hayes Shanesy
Production coordinated by Greg Nock

TABLE OF
CONTENTS

SCOPE

BOR 1-1 | Purpose

The Book of Rules (BOR) was established to outline acceptable practices and procedures in various social situations. Many everyday actions, while not illegal or immoral, are generally considered improper and are outlined within this handbook. This manual establishes and reinforces life rules required to be a productive member of American society.

A. The BOR is applicable to all citizens of the United States and all of its territories. Although not specifically mandated for citizens outside of the United States, most BOR regulations are generally accepted worldwide.

BOR 1-2 | Jurisdiction

State and federal law override this handbook whenever specific statutes contradict individual rules or requirements of the BOR. Good judgment shall be utilized when individual statutes are in question. Additionally, specific regulations may be contrary to the religious beliefs of an individual. In such cases, individual regulatory exclusions specific to religious beliefs are permissible.

A. Use common sense.

BOR I-3 | Reference

A copy of the BOR shall be kept readily available for reference at all home and work locations. BOR D-1 Discrepancy Forms (see Appendix A) shall also be readily available and may be utilized as required. Previous versions are obsolete and shall be replaced within thirty days of the effective date of updated publications.

BOR I-4 | Definition of Terms

SHALL implies an action, motion or procedure is mandatory.

MAY implies an action, motion or procedure is optional.

WILL implies a future action is mandatory.

INDIVIDUAL refers to a single person or group of people.

EXCEPTIONS detail situations in which a specific BOR regulation may be ignored. Exceptions are generally not inclusive, and good judgment shall be exercised when considering exceptions not detailed in this manual.

PHRASEOLOGY EXAMPLE details verbatim phrases required—or acceptable phrases allowable—in various situations.

BOR I-5 | Discrepancy Forms

All American adults have a primary responsibility to issue BOR D-1 Discrepancy Forms to individuals when violations to the

BOR are personally observed. No other action is warranted or required. The violator alone has the specific requirement to ensure that corrective measures will be taken to become compliant with the BOR.

A. The BOR D-1 Discrepancy Form is located in Appendix A of this publication.

B. Additional BOR D-1 Discrepancy Forms may be ordered at www.thebookofrules.com.

BOR I-6 | Authorized Deviations

Individual exclusions from any regulation contained within *The Book of Rules* are permissible whenever compliance with this manual may jeopardize the safety of others. The phrase "Safety Exception" followed by the specific BOR regulation violated shall be clearly expressed whenever a BOR regulation is intentionally violated in the presence of others.

PHRASEOLOGY EXAMPLE: *"Safety Exception 3-1"*

NOTE: Local and regional customs or procedures may warrant deviations from individual regulations contained within the BOR. Prior to implementing formal individual or organizational exclusions, permission shall be obtained from the BOR Regulatory Board at www.thebookofrules.com.

BOR I-7 | Submissions

Unsolicited submissions regarding amendments and additions to the BOR are encouraged. Changes may be proposed in writing by completing the BOR S-1 Submission Form (see Appendix B) or online at www.thebookofrules.com. Submissions become the property of the BOR Regulatory Board after receipt and will not be returned. The inclusion decision will be determined solely by the BOR Regulatory Board.

DRIVING

| BOR 2-1 | **Crossing the Path of a Vehicle**

Pedestrians crossing the path of a motor vehicle shall make personal eye contact with the driver prior to initiating passage across the path of the vehicle. If eye contact is not initiated, the driver of the vehicle is warranted to honk the horn, yell loudly and aggressively wave his or her fist. Vulgarity is only authorized when a violating pedestrian is operating a cell phone (see BOR 11-8 C).

A. Pedestrians more than halfway across the street when a vehicle approaches are not required to initiate eye contact with drivers.

| BOR 2-2 | **Limiting Unnecessary Driving**

Driving a motorized vehicle is only authorized when the distance between the departure and destination location exceeds 200 yards. Driving "across the street" and other needless trips are considered excessive and wasteful. Unnecessary driving contributes to obesity and wastes fuel.

BOR 2-1. Pedestrians crossing the path of a motor vehicle shall make personal eye contact with the driver prior to initiating passage across the path of the vehicle.

A. Allowable vehicle operations less than 200 yards:

1. Moderate or greater precipitation is currently occurring (see BOR 4-16 A1a).

2. Physical restrictions of the driver or any passenger prohibit walking.

3. A song, program or talk show warrants additional listening.

4. The transport of heavy objects would make walking impractical.

5. The movement of a vehicle is required for maintenance of said vehicle.

BOR 2-3 | The Green Light Honk

When stopped at a red light behind one or more vehicles, all vehicles ahead of a driver are allowed 3 seconds to accelerate after the light turns green. Honking the horn is permitted and encouraged after the mandatory 3-second wait period has expired. After any vehicle initiates a "Green Light Honk," successive honks are forbidden unless an additional 3 seconds have passed since the previous "Green Light Honk."

BOR 2-4 | The Hang-Up Honk

Except when expressly forbidden by law, it is allowable to place and receive cell phone calls while driving. Texting while driving is always prohibited (see BOR 11-12 B). Cell phone driving

BOR 2-4. Cell phone driving is permissible for the operator of any motorized vehicle until a mandatory suspension is required after receiving a "Hang-Up Honk."

is permissible for the operator of any motorized vehicle until a mandatory suspension is required after receiving a "Hang-Up Honk." This honk may be initiated by the driver of any motor vehicle who observes the unsafe driving practices of a cell phone driver (see BOR 11-8 D).

A. Immediately after the receipt of a "Hang-Up Honk," cell phone drivers shall abruptly cease conversation with the verbatim cell phone termination phrase below.

PHRASEOLOGY EXAMPLE: *"I've been HONKED; I have to go."*

BOR 2-5 | The Right Turn Honk

In an effort to decrease traffic congestion, all U.S. states allow a right turn at a red light after a complete stop. A right turn at a red light is authorized unless a "No Turn on Red" sign is clearly posted. Drivers shall vigilantly look both ways before turning into a lane of traffic. Some vehicles, such as a school bus or a HAZMAT vehicle, are prohibited from turning right at a red light.

A. When stopped at a red light behind a vehicle in a right turn lane, drivers are authorized to make the "Right Turn Honk" at the preceding vehicle when no traffic is observed in the perpendicular lane. The "Right Turn Honk" consists of two quick honks of the automobile horn.

BOR 2-6 | Discouraging Tailgaters

Tailgating is defined as following so closely to another vehicle that a collision may not be avoided. Tailgating is typically conducted unconsciously, or due to a perceived lack of risk. Accomplished by aggressive drivers, tailgating is a contributing factor in most motor vehicle accidents. The deliberate form of tailgating known as *slipstreaming* is illegal and dangerous. Slipstreaming is the practice of intentionally tailgating a large vehicle to reduce wind resistance, thereby enhancing fuel efficiency by as much as 10 percent.

A. Requesting that a following vehicle cease tailgating may be accomplished by initiating a tailgate termination request. This may be done in one of two ways:

   1. Slowing down

   2. Utilizing the windshield wiper fluid continually to spray the following vehicle

B. Both tailgate termination request options are permissible until a mandatory suspension is required after observing a tailgate flash. A tailgate flash is the flashing of the headlights by a tailgater to indicate acknowledgment of the violation and the intention to cease following too closely.

BOR 2-7 | Ensuring Children Are Safe and Occupied

Every effort shall be made to ensure children ride safely in motor vehicles. On average, three children die every day in vehicle accidents in the United States. It is the responsibility of a child's parents to ensure a vehicle is equipped with the proper car seat or booster chair. It is the responsibility of every adult passenger to ensure all children remain restrained while riding in a motor vehicle. The following requirements help ensure children remain safe, orderly and entertained while riding in a motor vehicle.

A. With the exception of baby bottles for infants, the consumption of food or water in a vehicle is prohibited for children under age twelve for all trips less than 30 minutes in duration.

BOR 2-7. Children's automobile activities, such as pulling the fist downward to request that a truck driver honk the horn, are encouraged.

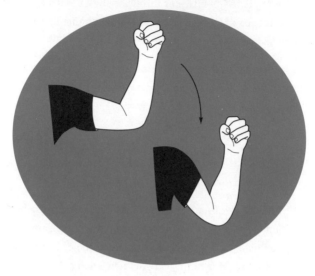

B. A collection of at least 3 hours of prerecorded children's music shall be permanently stored in vehicles in which children under age twelve routinely ride.

C. Children under eighteen who speak or sing at a level of 80 decibels or higher shall be instructed to remain silent for one hour, or the remaining duration of the trip, whichever is shorter.

D. Children's automobile activities, such as such as pulling the fist downward to request that a truck driver honk the horn, are encouraged.

| BOR 2-8 | **Singing Along With the Radio** |

When automobile options allow drivers to preprogram favorite radio stations into car stereos, all available channels shall be set to radio stations of the primary driver's preferred genre. This is accomplished to avoid the unnecessary listening of music or talk radio considered distasteful by the driver. The ability to rapidly change radio stations after an unpleasant song begins to play may help to avert a potentially hazardous driving situation.

A. Whenever an automobile passenger begins singing along with a song on the radio, the singer shall be allowed to continue singing until the completion of the song. Regardless of the quality of the singing, the driver may not change the radio station whenever all three of the following conditions exist.

   1. The singer must be moderately knowledgeable of the song lyrics.

   2. The song is not outside of the genre of the driver's musical taste.

   3. The singer continues to sing throughout the entire song.

B. The "Don't Change the Station, I'm Singing" option may only be exercised twice each hour by any individual in a moving motor vehicle (see BOR 2-9).

BOR 2-9 | Control of Dashboard Configurations

The driver of a motor vehicle, alone, has exclusive control of all dashboard controls, including radio configuration and climate settings. This privilege may be delegated to any passenger after verbal coordination has been established.

A. Passengers of any age who are guilty of three or more configuration violations in a seven-day period shall lose front seat privileges for a period designated by the driver, not to exceed thirty days. A configuration violation is defined as the manipulation of any dashboard control without verbal approval from the driver.

B. Passengers in vehicles with separate dashboard controls may adjust controls without permission from the driver.

BOR 2-10 **Proper Parking Alignment**

While parking a vehicle, care should be taken to ensure the vehicle is centered between the white parking lines. No portion of the vehicle may be within 10 inches of a white line. Whenever measuring devices are not available, 10 inches may be estimated. If it is determined that a vehicle is outside of parking tolerance, the vehicle shall be immediately repositioned.

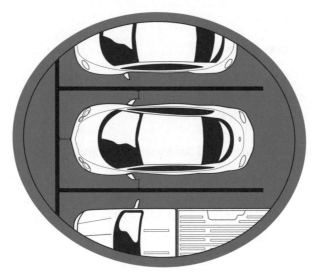

BOR 2-10. While parking a vehicle, no portion of the vehicle may be within 10 inches of a white line.

A. Whenever parking large vehicles that prohibit the 10 inch buffer, two or more parking spaces shall be utilized.

   1. Owners of RVs and other large vehicles should exercise thoughtfulness by parking toward the rear of the parking lot, when feasible.

B. Groups traveling in multiple vehicles are excluded from the 10-inch restriction between other individual vehicles within the group. The 10-inch restriction applies between vehicles within the group and other vehicles in the lot.

C. Drivers experiencing engine problems of any variety are exempt from BOR 2-10. Motorists are allowed a reasonable amount of time to correct engine problems before repositioning is required.

BOR 2-11 | Stopping During Parking

For the purpose of obtaining a premium parking spot, stopping a vehicle in a parking lane to wait for a parked vehicle to exit a spot is forbidden. Stopping in a lane significantly impedes the flow of traffic and delays vehicles entering and exiting the lot. Individuals desiring a premium parking location shall slowly circle in a lot until a premium spot becomes available.

A. When brake lights are observed on a parked vehicle preparing to exit a parking spot, a brief stop of thirty seconds or less is permitted to wait for the parking spot.

B. Whenever unusual circumstances exist or severe weather is occurring, drivers may wait a reasonable amount of time in a parking lane for a premium parking location.

1. Severe weather is defined as any meteorological condition in which driving at a speed in excess of fifty-five miles per hour would be considered unsafe.

C. Drivers stopped in a parking lane waiting for the parking spot of an exiting vehicle shall turn on the vehicle turn signal to indicate intentions.

BOR 2-12 | Reserved Vehicle Seating

A single individual shall be designated as the primary driver for every vehicle in the home. Passengers who routinely ride with the primary driver may be assigned a specific seat in individual vehicles. Reserved riders are authorized to store up to three personal items in vehicles, such as sunglasses, headphones and cell phone chargers. Personal items shall be stored in a nonvisible car location when not in use.

A. Guest passengers shall ride in a nonreserved seat when traveling with reserved passengers.

B. Social conversation is required by all riders when initiated by the primary driver. The uncomfortable silence often experienced between the driver and a guest passenger may be broken by either individual by asking a polite ice-breaker question.

PHRASEOLOGY EXAMPLE: *"Hey Steve, thanks a lot for the ride. You are really a lifesaver after my car broke down. But I was just curious: Did you know you could actually fit four people in your car if you shoveled all of your fast-food trash off the backseat?"*

BOR 2-13 | Authorized Personalized License Plates

Personalized license plates, or *vanity plates*, are license plates with a preselected set of letters and numbers that have special meaning to the individual who registers the motor vehicle. Personalized license plates cost significantly more than license plates with random digits and serve as a significant source of revenue for many states.

A. Although expensive, personalized license plates are recommended for all individuals. The automobile usually reflects one's personality, and the license plate is intentionally placed in an area of high visibility. Spread your message to the world.

B. Personalized license plates are prohibited if the message cannot be clearly understood by at least 50 percent of the local population. For example, the personalized license plate "IWTRWJL" is not authorized.

   1. Proposed personalized license plates shall be reviewed by at least nine co-workers, friends or relatives. License plate proposals shall be reconsidered if less than 50 percent understand the intended meaning.

DOR 2-14 | Car Washing Recommendations

The outward appearance and cleanliness of an automobile reflects the hygiene of an individual. Frequent car washing helps ensure the longevity of the paint. The use of automated car washes is authorized, but the preferred method of washing the car is always hand washing. Vehicle exteriors shall be washed at least monthly, but it is recommended that exterior car washing is accomplished biweekly. Vehicle interiors, including dashboards and carpet, shall be cleaned at least once every four months.

BOR 2-14. Writing the phrase "Wash Me" with a fingertip on excessively dirty vehicles is authorized, if not previously accomplished by another individual.

A. Households with children between the ages of ten and eighteen shall assign the chore of car washing to the oldest child.

B. Writing the phrase "Wash Me" with a fingertip on excessively dirty vehicles is authorized, if not previously accomplished by another individual.

BOR 2-15 | Unlocking Car Doors

The driver of a motor vehicle traveling with passengers shall ensure all vehicle doors are unlocked before the engine is engaged. Individuals waiting outside a locked car hearing the engine engage may become severely depressed, facing the possibility of abandonment. One out of nine divorced individuals cited "AAA"—Automobile Abandonment Anxiety—as one of the top three reasons for the separation.

A. Passengers locked outside of a parked vehicle with the engine engaged may shout and knock loudly on doors and windows.

PHRASEOLOGY EXAMPLE: *"Hey! Did you forget about somebody, Coach?"*

1. Vulgarity is permissible only when severe weather is currently occurring (see BOR 2-11 B 1).

B. When remote control door unlocking is not available, vehicle doors shall be unlocked in the following order.

1. Driver Door
2. Passenger Door
3. Right Rear Door
4. Left Rear Door

BOR 2-16 | First Car Selection

Extreme care should be taken in the selection of an individual's first car. All future car purchases will be compared to the first-car experience. First-time automobile buyers almost always have a limited budget. Therefore, care should be taken to select a first-time automobile that is safe, fuel efficient and stylish.

A. Along with mother's maiden name and city of birth, the make and model of an individual's first car is often a password security question on secure websites. For that reason, first-time buyers should select first cars with an easily remembered and simply spelled name. For example, a Chevy Nova is a preferred first vehicle over a Maserati Quattroporte.

B. Shortly after the purchase of an individual's first car, a single car charm shall be chosen for the vehicle. Selected car charms shall be either placed on the dashboard or hung from

BOR 2-16. Selected car charms shall be either placed on the dashboard or hung from the rearview mirror.

the rearview mirror. Car charms may include, but are not limited to, fuzzy dice, photographs and plastic green frogs.

1. After the purchase of a new vehicle, car charms shall be either moved to the new vehicle or replaced with another charm.

BOR 2-17 | Proper Use of GPS Devices

Global positioning systems provide an accurate vehicle position from signals received from stationary satellites. A GPS allows drivers to travel to unfamiliar destinations without the use of a road map. GPS is a recommended option in all vehicles. Although a powerful tool, GPS receivers should only serve as a reference and may not be completely accurate. Care should always be taken to be cognizant of one's surroundings while driving.

A. Mobile GPS devices shall be stored in the vehicle glove box when not in use to prevent theft.

B. Manipulating GPS configurations is forbidden without verbal approval from the driver.

C. Many individuals assign a name to the voice of their personal GPS device and speak to it directly. This practice is authorized provided direct verbal communication is not conducted in the presence of others.

   1. Suggested names for GPS devices include Jeeves, Alfred, Penelope and Martha.

D. Blindly following GPS instructions that have proven incorrect is prohibited. Both female and male drivers shall stop and ask directions whenever necessary.

BOR 2-18 | Citing Violating Drivers

BOR D-1 Discrepancy Forms (see Appendix A) issued to violating drivers shall be thoroughly and accurately completed and placed under the driver's side windshield wiper. Citations shall be issued in accordance with BOR 1-5. Additional actions and confrontations with violating drivers are prohibited.

3

SHOPPING

BOR 3-1 Shopping Mall Flow of Pedestrian Traffic

The flow of pedestrian traffic shall be counterclockwise in the common areas of shopping malls. This standardizes the flow of movement within the mall. All individuals shall enter the proper flow of traffic as quickly as practicable after entering the mall or exiting individual stores within the mall.

A. Shoppers with disabilities are exempt from the counterclockwise requirement, if moving against the flow of traffic provides an operational advantage.

B. The standardized walking rate is between three and six miles per hour. Passing slower shoppers shall always be accomplished on the left.

C. Stopping to window shop or slowing to a speed less than three miles per hour shall always be accomplished to the right of the flow of pedestrian traffic.

BOR 3-1. The flow of pedestrian traffic shall be counterclockwise in the common areas of shopping malls. This standardizes the flow of movement.

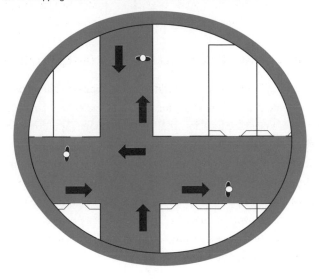

BOR 3-2 | Maximum Allowable Shopping Times

The maximum allowable shopping times at malls and other large shopping locations vary due to gender differences between men and women. The practice of shopping should never be hurried and shall be accomplished purposefully. In an effort to reduce loitering, time limits were established in 2008 based on the gender of a shopping party. Nonshopping activities such as "mall walking" are permitted, provided activities are accomplished with intent, and time restrictions are honored.

A. Maximum Shopping Mall Time Chart

    1. One or more male shoppers: 2 hours

    2. One or more female shoppers: 3 hours

    3. A group of males and females: 2 hours and 30 minutes

B. Time extensions are allowable in 30-minute increments, if at least one purchase is made in each extension, regardless of the gender of the shopping party.

BOR 3-3 │ Establishing Designated Meeting Locations

Groups of individuals who separate while shopping shall establish a predetermined meeting location and designated time. The designated meeting location shall be convenient for all individuals in a shopping party. Factors such as parking location, distance to preferred stores and proximity to eating establishments shall be considered in determining the optimal meeting location. Parties more than 15 minutes late at meeting locations shall be considered overdue. Overdue individuals may be excluded in future mall visits and shopping outings, if a justifiable excuse for tardiness does not exist.

BOR 3-4 │ Mall Familiarization Exercises

The entrance used on the initial visit to a mall or large shopping complex shall also be used on successive shopping visits. Utilizing the same entrance increases mall spatial awareness and reduces the likelihood of mall disorientation. As familiarity gradually increases, individuals may more effectively accomplish shopping goals within the prescribed maximum shopping time limits (see BOR 3-2).

A. This practice shall be exercised until all individuals within a shopping group achieve shopping mall familiarization.

1. Shopping mall familiarization is defined as having the ability to provide a general location of 75 percent or more stores within a shopping complex.

BOR 3-5 | Shopping Cart Selection and Return

The selection of the shopping cart shall be made by the adult member of a shopping party who is closest to the shopping cart row. In a shopping party comprised entirely of individuals under the age of eighteen, shopping cart selection shall be accomplished by the oldest member of the party. Care should be taken to ensure a cart with properly operating wheels is selected. Sanitary wipes, when provided, shall be used to clean the cart handle and other areas of the cart as desired.

A. Shopping carts shall never be stopped in the center of an aisle. Carts shall be positioned sufficiently left or right of the aisle centerline to allow other carts to pass freely.

B. As with motor vehicles, the shopping cart on the right at an aisle intersection has the right of way.

 1. Shopping cart priority in ascending order is given to:

    a. Shoppers With Children
    b. Disabled Shoppers
    c. Pregnant Shoppers
    d. Elderly Shoppers
    e. Armed Shoppers

 2. Ties shall be broken by the most aggressive shopper.

C. Shoppers of any age are permitted to ride in the cart, provided horseplay is not conducted.

D. Shopping carts shall be either returned to the entryway of shopping facilities or placed in cart return receptacles after use. If the cart return location is 100 yards or more from the parked vehicle, the driver shall pick up the cart return

BOR 3-5. As with motor vehicles, the shopping cart on the right at an aisle intersection has the right of way.

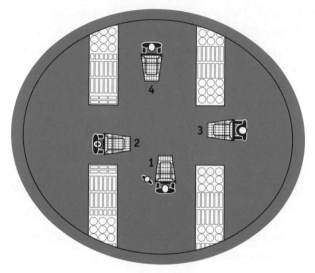

designee. Whenever moderate or greater precipitation is occurring (see BOR 4-16 A1a), the cart return designee shall be picked up regardless of the distance between the vehicle and cart return location.

1. The selection of the cart return designee shall be determined in this order:

    a. Children able to accomplish the task unsupervised

    b. Passengers of motor vehicle riding in a rear seat

    c. Passengers of motor vehicle riding in the front passenger seat

    d. The driver of the motor vehicle

BOR 3-6 | Avoiding Unnecessary Conversation

During the checkout process, only necessary conversation directly related to the transaction is permissible. The responsibility of expediting the transactional process lies with both the customer and the cashier. Prompt, polite statements such as "hello" and "thank you" are permissible, provided such statements do not develop into actual conversation.

A. While checking out, small talk such as "What do you think about the weather?," "Did you see the news today?" or "Did you see what the news said about the weather today?" is strictly forbidden.

NOTE: It is rumored that shortly before the assassination of President Lincoln, Ulysses S. Grant was delayed in his visit to Ford's Theatre due to a lengthy shopping visit. While in line at the Towne Goods Mercantile, clerk Anna Thomas began discussing with Grant the details surrounding the divorce affairs of one Thomas Smithers. This small talk delayed Mr. Grant's arrival by 26 minutes and may have contributed to the assassination of one of the greatest presidents in American history.

BOR 3-7 | The Primary Household Shopper

A single individual in every group of cohabitating adults will be designated as the primary household shopper. Along with paying the bills and maintaining the lawn, ensuring the home is well stocked with food is one of the most important duties in the home. The primary shopper is responsible for ensuring the home is stocked with 50 percent or more of the desired meals and snacks for the following seven days. Household food

BOR 3-7. A dynamic shopping list containing required and requested food should be maintained on the kitchen refrigerator.

supplies shall be generally representative of the collective desired foods of the adult residents.

A. The primary shopper or authorized designee shall shop for groceries whenever the collective desired household food supply falls below 50 percent.

B. A dynamic shopping list containing required and requested food should be maintained on the kitchen refrigerator (See BOR 9-7).

1. The primary shopper will objectively consider the food requests of all household residents based on nutrition and the household budget.

C. The primary shopper is the ultimate authority in selecting the specific brands of all food items purchased for the home.

1. Individuals personally selected by the primary shopper to purchase groceries in their absence hold all rights and privileges of the primary shopper. This includes, but is not limited to, prioritizing purchases from grocery lists and brand discretion, regardless of previous purchases.

D. Although primary shoppers have historically been female, the position may be held by any man, woman or child over age twelve in the home.

BOR 3-8 | The Self-Checkout Line

Self-checkout devices are automated machines that allow customers to scan and pay for items without human interaction. Self-checkout lines are most common in department stores and large grocery stores. Since their inception in 1992, self-checkout lines have become available at most major retailers across the country. However, the disadvantages of using self-checkout lines far outweigh the advantages. The promoted time efficiency of self-checkout lines depends on the shoppers' familiarity with the devices. The self-checkout line has resulted in the loss of thousands of jobs due to automation and has made shopping into a significantly less personal event. Further, self-checkout lines promote shoplifting, which negates the cost benefit of their operation.

A. Self-checkout lines shall not be used.

BOR 3-9 | Seasonal Shopping Guidelines

Seasonal items such as Easter baskets and Christmas tree ornaments shall be purchased only as prescribed in the Seasonal Shopping Chart. Purchasing seasonal items outside of the shopping window encourages merchants to display groups of items out of season. Such practices reduce the significance of the current holiday season.

A. Seasonal Shopping Chart

NEW YEAR'S DAY	Dec 15th – Jan 1st
VALENTINE'S DAY	Feb 1st – Feb 14th
ST. PATRICK'S DAY	March 11th – March 18th
EASTER	Two weeks prior to Easter Sunday
U.S. INDEPENDENCE DAY	June 20th – July 6th
HALLOWEEN	Any day in October
THANKSGIVING	Nov 1st – Thanksgiving
CHRISTMAS	Nov 15th – Dec 31st

B. Purchasing seasonal items outside of the appropriate seasonal window is allowable only:

1. When purchasing clearance items for the following year

2. When shoppers are physically or financially unable to purchase items within the seasonal window

BOR 3-10 | Shopping With Children

Parents and guardians shall make every effort to ensure children are well behaved while shopping. Unruly children at shopping centers may cause an unpleasant and occasionally hazardous shopping experience for others. Supervising children shall be the primary priority of parents while shopping.

BOR 3-10. Children under age twelve shall never be outside the visual range of parents while shopping.

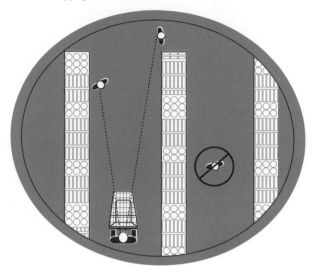

The following four procedures shall be enforced at all times by parents while shopping.

A. Children under age twelve shall never be outside the visual range of parents while shopping.

B. Children may not walk or run at such speeds that would endanger other shoppers.

C. Parents must make every effort to soothe crying children to avoid hindering the shopping experience of others.

   1. If parents are unable to suppress extreme noise from children, the child or children shall be removed from the shopping establishment within five minutes.

D. Children are prohibited from wearing wheeled shoes while shopping.

BOR 3-11 | Protocol After Finding Money

Finding money on the ground is a gift from heaven. Small change and occasionally currency can be found almost anywhere while shopping. A found nickel or quarter may not sound like much, but over time, discovered small change can add up. However, discovering small change while shopping really isn't about the money. Luck is a fairly intangible thing, but a small portion of luck is bestowed into your life with each discovered coin.

A. A small portion of an individual's positional awareness should be dedicated to the discovery of change or currency while shopping.

B. If the individual who dropped the change or currency can easily be determined, returning the money is mandatory.

C. Every individual in a six-figure household shall, at one point in their life, intentionally drop currency in the amount of $20 or more to be discovered by another shopper.

   1. Anonymously waiting to discover the recipient of the dropped currency gift is discouraged, although not prohibited.

D. Individuals shopping with young children are encouraged to discreetly drop a few coins on the ground while checking out. This serves two purposes. It keeps children occupied in the checkout line and prevents their wandering eyes from discovering candy bars and other items children often pester parents to purchase.

BOR 3-12 | Protecting Personal Information

Regardless of method, every shopping transaction discloses some personal information. Identity thieves thrive on careless individuals who unintentionally reveal private data while shopping. Identity theft occurs when someone obtains enough private information to open an account or make purchases in your name. Every effort should be made to limit the amount of personal information revealed while shopping.

A. Debit card PIN numbers shall be entered discreetly using the palm of the hand to disguise keypad entries.

B. Paper receipts should always be shredded or destroyed.

C. Paying for purchases with the use of a personal check is discouraged. Checks usually contain your name, address and phone number.

D. A growing number of retailers require or request personal information with purchases. The disclosed purpose of this practice is the compilation of statistical information for direct marketing programs. In today's society, privacy is a commodity that must be protected. Fictitious personal information shall be provided when prompted.

   1. When personal information is requested to complete a purchase, the following fictitious data shall be provided:

   Name: George Glass (male shoppers); Wendy Peffercorn (female shoppers)

   E-Mail Address: elo@thebookofrules.com

   Zip Code: 63025

BOR 3-12. Debit card PIN numbers shall be entered discreetly using the palm of the hand to disguise keypad entries.

Phone Number: 642.867.5309

NOTE: The telephone number 867-5309 is referenced in the 1980's song "Jenny" by Tommy Tutone. 642 is an unused area code.

BOR 3-13 | Purchasing Lottery Tickets

State lotteries are generally offered in one of two varieties: the "scratch off" ticket and the general lottery. Often disguised as a socially responsible institution that funds education, state lotteries allow state legislators to divert funding intended for education to other programs with the revenue generated from losing lottery tickets. State lotteries are generally considered discriminatory as they serve as a tax on the ignorant and individuals with poor math skills.

A. Whenever one or more shoppers are in line behind an individual, the purchase of lottery tickets is restricted to $5 or less.

B. Regardless of the jackpot amount, the weekly purchase of lottery tickets may not exceed 1 percent of an individual's weekly gross income.

   NOTE: The purchase of a lottery ticket only slightly increases the odds of winning a major jackpot.

C. The purchase of lottery tickets is considered voluntary taxation and is generally discouraged unless one of three situations occurs:

   1. Currency is found that meets or exceeds the purchase price of a lottery ticket.

   2. An unpaid lottery ticket is discovered at the checkout counter.

   3. Numbers revealed in a dream specifically correspond to a current lottery game.

BOR 3-14 | Expeditiously Checking Out

Shoppers should choose the checkout lane with the smallest line. Additional factors including exit proximity, lines with children and coupon shopper avoidance shall be considered before a checkout lane in selected. Prior to lane selection, all shopping lanes shall be briefly scanned for the possible availability of a "no wait" line. The checkout process shall be executed as expeditiously as practical.

A. Express lanes with maximum allowable items clearly posted shall be utilized only by shoppers with an appropriate

BOR 3-14. Shoppers should choose the checkout lane with the smallest line. Additional factors shall be considered before a checkout lane in selected.

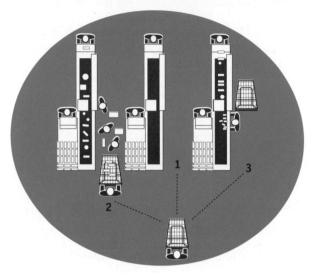

number of items. Entering a "twelve items or less" lane with more than twelve items is an offense that shall be treated with the severity of similar crimes, such as shoplifting and verbal assault.

B. The practice of paying for merchandise with change, except for fast food, is permissible without restriction (see BOR 4-15), up to a maximum of $9.99. However, paying with change delays the checkout process and is strongly discouraged.

C. The intention to use more than five coupons shall be clearly disclosed to all shoppers in line.

D. Bagging purchases is discouraged whenever two items or less are purchased.

E. Whenever practical, shoppers should bring their own bag for purchases.

1. Most states allow this practice to legally count as a fulfilled New Year's resolution for the following year.

4

DINING OUT

Restaurant Dress Codes

Clothing worn in restaurants shall be appropriate to the category of the eating establishment. If you are unsure about the dress code of a restaurant, verify the requirements before arriving. Restaurant types and corresponding dress codes are divided into four classes.

A. Class A restaurants consist of any restaurant that offers either valet parking or maître d' services (or both) or any restaurant in which the average entrée price meets or exceeds $50. These establishments require formal wear of any variety.

B. Class B restaurants include all restaurants not covered by Class A in which seating is determined by a host or hostess. These establishments require business casual dress.

C. Class C restaurants consist of all restaurants not covered by Class A, B or D. These establishments require clean clothing.

D. Class D restaurants consist of any eating establishment that offers either a value meal or self-service drinks. Class D restaurants also include any restaurant that conducts 25 percent or more of its total business at a drive-through window. These establishments require a minimum of shoes and a shirt be worn, simultaneously, for the entire duration of the meal.

BOR 4-2 | Tipping Guidelines

As referenced in BOR 8-1 A, tipping food delivery specialists is one of the three areas in life in which individuals are encouraged to splurge monetarily. Waiters and waitresses typically earn less than one-third of the minimum wage and depend upon customer-generated compensation for their livelihood. Tips shall be calculated as a percentage of the total food bill including tax. The exact amount of an appropriate tip varies due to a number of circumstances but should range from 10 percent for substandard service to 20 percent or more for exceptional service.

A. Verbal compliments shall never be offered in lieu of a tip. In the case of non-availability of funds for an appropriate tip, a simple apologetic phrase shall be offered to the server.

B. If confronted by a server with the question, "Do you want change?" the Change Response Phrase shall be immediately offered, and one dollar shall be deducted from the tip.

   PHRASEOLOGY EXAMPLE: *"No, I like the way I am. Thank you."*

C. The absolute minimum tip, regardless of the quality of service, is one dollar. Whenever the minimum tip of one dollar is offered for meals in excess of ten dollars, the reason shall be clearly communicated to the server. This may be accomplished verbally or by placing a polite note on the table after the check has been paid.

BOR 4-3 | Acknowledging Acquaintances

Often when dining at public establishments, friends, family or co-workers may be observed. It is forbidden to join another party's table unless verbal permission is first obtained. The seated party has the sole authority to initiate a seating invitation, if desired. Under no circumstances may a standing individual solicit an invitation by asking, "May I join you?" or similar phrases.

A. Loitering nearby an acquaintance's table or repeatedly attempting to initiate conversation to prompt a seating invitation is prohibited.

B. A seated party not desiring to be joined by a persistent standing party may take the following action. A polite smile shall be directed at the standing party, to make eye contact. The right pointer and middle finger shall be extended together, pointing slightly left or right of the standing party.

NOTE: The standing party will interpret the action as follows: "Thank you for taking the time to stop by our table to speak with us. However, we are currently engaged in personal conversation and respectfully ask for privacy. If you wish to communicate with us at a later date, please do not hesitate to call. Your cooperation in this matter is greatly appreciated."

BOR 4-3. The right pointer and middle finger shall be extended together, pointing slightly left or right of the standing party.

BOR 4-4 | Special Event Dining

Special event dining is defined as participating in a recreational meal with one or more individuals, with the primary purpose being to celebrate a specific event, milestone or achievement. Qualifying special events include birthdays, anniversaries or any other event that would justify the purchase of a greeting card. The coordination of unannounced celebratory procedures, such as wait staff singing "Happy Birthday" or making an announcement is authorized only after verbal approval has been obtained from the celebrating individual or individuals.

A. The selection of the special event dining location shall be determined by the individual celebrating the event.

B. If the woman celebrating falls between the age of 30 and 65, her age shall not be disclosed.

C. A party celebrating a special event is exempt from BOR 4-8 B.

BOR 4-5 | Touching Hot Plates

Men over the age of twelve who touch hot plates at restaurants after being warned of high temperatures shall not be scorned, ridiculed or disciplined. This is a male genetic defect, and no one knows exactly why it occurs.

BOR 4-6 | Dining Out With Coupons

Negative connotations are often associated with the use of coupons at dining facilities. Restaurants provide coupons to

BOR 4-5. Men over the age of twelve who touch hot plates at restaurants after being warned of high temperatures exhibit a male genetic defect.

promote themselves in a competitive marketplace. Coupons are allowable at Class B, C and D restaurants (see BOR 4-1) without restriction. Paying with a coupon is permissible at Class A restaurants with the consent of all adult members of a dining party.

BOR 4-7 | The Restaurant Selector

One individual in a dining party shall be designated as the restaurant selector. The restaurant selector has the responsibility to expeditiously determine the dining location for a dining party. Except as outlined in BOR 4-4 A, restaurant selector rights shall be rotated regularly among all adults who routinely dine together. Restaurant selector rights may be designated to individuals under age eighteen with the collective consent of all adult members of a dining party.

A. The restaurant selector shall determine the dining location for a dining party within ten minutes after the decision to dine outside the home has been made.

B. The restaurant selector's restaurant determination shall be clearly and promptly communicated to all members of a dining party.

C. The restaurant selector's inability to determine a dining location within ten minutes constitutes failure and initiates the immediate transfer of restaurant selector rights to another individual.

BOR 4-8 | Proper Restaurant Seating

To minimize wait times at Class A and B restaurants (see BOR 4-1), reservations should be made in advance. The restaurant selector (see BOR 4-7) should check in with the host or hostess shortly after arriving at a restaurant. All individuals waiting for a table should ensure a clear path exists between the restaurant entrance and the host or hostess stand.

A. Cell phone conversation shall be limited to five minutes for seated individuals at Class A and B restaurants. Cell phones may be operated without restriction for individuals waiting to be seated at Class A and B restaurants, and at all times at Class C and D restaurants.

B. Whenever ten or more individuals are observed waiting for a table, seated dining parties shall exit the restaurant within fifteen minutes after the completion of the meal.

C. Individuals waiting for a table may personally address seated parties loitering after a meal.

> **PHRASEOLOGY EXAMPLE:** *"Hey Woody, I'm sure your friends would love to hear more about your game-winning high school touchdown after you've paid your check and left."*

BOR 4-9 | Sharing Food

Sharing food with other members of a dining party offers individuals an excellent opportunity to try new foods (see BOR 5-1). Concerns about germs and unfair food distribution may deter diners from sharing food with others. Yet when coordinated prior to the beginning of a meal, sharing food with others is sanitary and significantly enhances the dining experience. Increasing the variety of foods also improves the nutritional value of every meal.

A. Sharing food with others is optional after the beginning of a meal.

B. Directly reaching for food from another individual's plate without permission is prohibited.

1. Violators of BOR 4-9 B shall be reprimanded as such: by upwardly brushing away the violator's hand and making immediate eye contact.

2. Stabbing the hand of violators with a fork is socially impolite and illegal in most states.

C. Condiments such as ketchup and salsa shall never be applied directly to a shared appetizer or entrée without the expressed verbal consent of all members of a dining party.

D. The intention to share desserts with others shall be disclosed prior to the beginning of the meal.

1. There is a subtle difference between asking for a taste and sharing a dessert. This is generally self-explanatory.

BOR 4-9. Violators of BOR 4-9 B shall be reprimanded as such: by upwardly brushing away the violator's hand and making immediate eye contact.

Individuals who do not fully understand this concept are discouraged from eating outside of the home.

BOR 4-10 | Splitting the Check

General etiquette mandates that individuals who regularly dine together share in the responsibility of payment. The responsibly of restaurant payment has ended many relationships and shall be considered carefully. Taking turns paying the check is an acceptable alternative to splitting the check.

A. When splitting the check, an individual's total food bill rounded up to next dollar shall be offered to the paying individual. The additional amount shall be added to the server's tip.

B. A man shall always pay for dinner on the first date with a woman.

   1. Women shall offer to pay for dinner on a second date, and men shall refuse.

   2. Payment for future dinner dates shall be negotiated fairly based upon income, event and the progression of the relationship.

C. Mothers dining with adult children shall never pay for dinner.

BOR 4-11 | Dining With Children

The dining out experience consists of more than the consumption of food. Disruptive children hinder the dining experience for everyone. Every effort shall be made to ensure children are well behaved at restaurants. Keeping small children occupied during the meal assists in controlling behavior. Compressing the duration of the meal also helps accomplish this goal. Idle time often prompts children to misbehave. All adults dining with children have an equal responsibly of supervision. Well-behaved children foster a more pleasant dining experience for all diners.

A. Children under age twelve are prohibited from dining in Class A restaurants (see BOR 4-1 A).

B. The server's tip shall be increased by 5 percent if children are unruly or messy during the meal.

C. The check shall always be paid prior to completion of the meal when dining with children.

D. Parents of unruly children shall be issued a BOR D-1 Discrepancy Form in accordance with BOR 1-5.

BOR 4-12   The Restaurant Special

Restaurant entrées are often designated as "specials" to promote specific dishes. These items are generally prepared and served in greater quantities than other dishes. The word "special" should indicate that a discount from the regular menu price will be offered when ordered. However, frequently the word "special" indicates only that an item is promoted and no discount is applied.

A. An individual who discovers that the regular menu price has been charged for a meal advertised as a special may take any one of the following three actions:

1. An inordinate amount of unsorted small change may be utilized to pay for the check. A sufficient supply of pennies and nickels may be stored in the automobile glove box to accomplish this task, when necessary.

   NOTE: A server's tip should never be adversely affected based solely on the pricing of restaurant specials.

BOR 4-12. An inordinate amount of unsorted small change may be utilized to pay for the check when the wrong price has been charged for a meal.

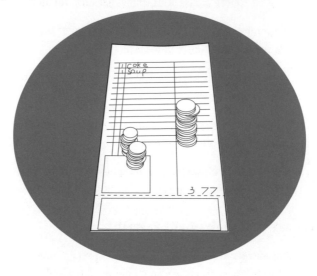

2. Restaurant management may be offered a "special" verbal statement after the completion of the meal.

3. A customer comment card may be sent postage due to restaurant management requesting a partial refund.

BOR 4-13 | Limiting Complimentary Items

Most restaurants offer free items with a meal. Free items range from toothpicks and breath mints to sourdough dinner rolls. Although advertised as free, nothing in life is truly free. The cost of free items is built into the price of items on the menu. Care should be taken not to take an excessive amount of any free item offered at restaurants.

A. Complimentary dinner items such as rolls and chips may be limitlessly requested by all adult patrons ordering an unshared entrée.

B. The total amount of complimentary after-dinner items such as toothpicks and mints taken from the cashier's counter should not exceed the holding capacity of pockets and purses.

| BOR 4-14 | **Fast-Food Line Priority**

When it is observed that any of the following corresponding food complements are missing from a completed fast-food order, individuals may immediately proceed to the front of the line to request the appropriate missing item. This will be accomplished by politely bypassing others currently in line and addressing employees directly.

A. Missing Fast-Food Item Priority Chart

FOOD ORDERED	MISSING ITEM
Any Entrée Requiring a Specific Utensil	Missing Item: Required Utensils
Hamburgers, Hot Dogs, French Fries	Missing Item: Ketchup
Mexican Food Item	Missing Item: Salsa
French Toast Sticks, Pancakes	Missing Item: Syrup
Iced Tea	Missing Item: Sweetener
Any Food Item	Missing Item: Napkin

BOR 4-14. When food complements are missing from a fast-food order, individuals may immediately proceed to the front of the line.

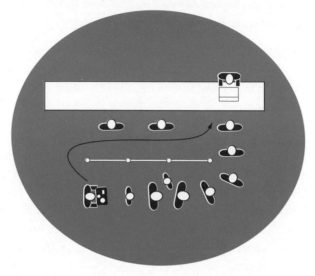

BOR 4-15 | Paying for Fast Food With Change

Paying for fast food with change is forbidden whenever a customer has other options for payment. All fast-food monetary transactions shall be completed as promptly as possible. Paying with change delays individuals in line behind a customer, confuses "currency impaired" cashiers, and delays the delivery of a meal.

A. Paying for fast food with change is allowable only when a dining patron has no other form of currency and all four of the following conditions exist:

1. No patrons are in line behind purchaser.

2. Change is organized and offered to the cashier expeditiously.

3. Distractions, such as small children, will not disturb the counting process.

4. Loud noises are avoided in the organization of coins.

B. Paying with change for all goods and services is permissible without restriction up to a maximum limit of $9.99 for all transactions except fast food (see BOR 3-14 B).

BOR 4-16 | Authorized Use of Drive-Through Windows

The use of drive-through windows is authorized only when three cars or fewer are currently in the drive-through line. Otherwise, the motor vehicle shall be parked in accordance with BOR 2-10, and ordering shall be accomplished inside the restaurant. This practice expedites the delivery of the meal. To the extent possible, individual fast-food selections shall be determined before a vehicle enters a drive-through line. Fast-food selections shall be clearly communicated to the driver before the vehicle is positioned at the ordering window. Food selection changes shall be kept to a minimum but are authorized with the nonavailability of desired menu items.

A. Allowable exceptions to enter a drive-through with four or more vehicles in line:

1. Precipitation of a moderate degree or greater is occurring.

    a. Moderate precipitation is defined as moisture landing on the windshield of a motor vehicle to such a degree that driving without wipers would be considered unsafe.

2. Physical restrictions exist with the driver or any passenger.

3. Driving patrons have a personal relationship with an individual working in the eating establishment's drive-through window.

   a. Personal conversation between patrons and restaurant staff are limited to sixty seconds whenever other vehicles are observed in line behind a vehicle.

4. The disturbance of an infant would be required to enter an eating establishment.

BOR 4-17 | Offering Compliments and Complaints

Restaurants depend on accurate patron feedback to ensure consistent quality service. Satisfied customers generally return to a restaurant after a pleasant dining experience. Complaints

BOR 4-17. An individual who makes more than two complaints in a calendar month should consider consulting a licensed therapist to discuss their inability to interact with others.

and compliments are typically offered for inferior or superior food quality or price, restaurant cleanliness, service and environmental conditions. Complaints should always be realistic; servers and chefs are human too. Feedback should generally be conducted privately and politely, and shall always be given after the completion of a meal.

A. Feedback shall always be offered directly to the acting manager and should be honest, specific and fair.

B. Servers should be evaluated on service and never on the quality of the food.

C. A server's tip may not be negatively impacted for not honoring an environmental request (too loud, too bright, etc.). Environmental conditions are almost always mandated by restaurant management.

D. An individual who makes more than two complaints in a calendar month should consider consulting a licensed therapist to discuss his or her inability to interact with others.

5

FOOD

BOR 5-1 **Trying New Foods**

Discovering new delicacies enhances the enjoyment of life. The standard American diet consists of only several dozen specific types of food. Enjoying new entrées can improve an individual's diet and can make life more interesting. Food neophobia, the fear of trying new foods, affects everyone to varying degrees. Overcoming this fear may result in the discovery of new favorite dishes. A simple way to sample a large number of new foods is to visit an ethnic buffet. Trying new ethnic dishes is like traveling to unfamiliar countries without worrying about currency conversion or automobile theft.

A. When presented with an entrée not previously tasted, an individual is required to take at least one bite.

   1. After the one-bite requirement has been met, undesired entrées are not required to be consumed. Along with voting, driving and running with scissors, "not

consuming disliked foods" is a constitutional right of all adult Americans.

BOR 5-2 | Accommodating Vegetarians

Vegetarians do not consume meat. Strict vegetarians, called vegans, also exclude foods that may contain animal by-products, such as cheese and milk. Vegetarians obtain necessary nutrients and proteins from other sources such as vegetables, nuts and grain. Considered a healthy alternative lifestyle, vegetarian diets contain significantly lower amounts of saturated fats and cholesterol. Vegetarians choose this lifestyle for a variety of ethical and health reasons.

A. A reasonable supply of nonmeat foods shall be maintained if one or more known vegetarians reside in the home.

1. A visiting vegetarian houseguest staying four days or longer is considered a temporary resident.

B. Meals prepared in the home for a vegetarian should include at least two nonmeat food items.

C. Derogatory nicknames, such as "Tofu," may not be directed at vegetarians.

D. Vegetarian food items may not be referenced as "twigs and berries," "rabbit food" or similar names in the presence of a known or suspected vegetarian.

E. The observance of a known vegetarian consuming meat shall be treated similarly to an alcoholic observed consuming alcohol. Interventions are authorized and encouraged under severe carnivorous circumstances.

Ketchup Placement

Ketchup (also spelled *catsup*) is a tomato-based condiment usually served with hamburgers, hot dogs and french fries. Although generally a healthful condiment, ketchup does not count as a daily serving of vegetables. When applying ketchup to a dinner plate, care should be taken to ensure ketchup is placed on the side of food.

A. French fries and similar food items shall never be smothered with ketchup. The practice of drowning a food item with any condiment, including ketchup, reflects the inferior intelligence of the eater. Violators observed by other eaters shall be promptly and courteously corrected.

BOR 5-3. When applying ketchup to a dinner plate, care should be taken to ensure ketchup is placed on the side of food.

B. Ketchup is a protected class condiment at fast-food restaurants. If it is discovered that hamburgers, hot dogs or french fries are not accompanied by ketchup, immediate line priority is justified (see BOR 4-14).

BOR 5-4 | **Taco Ingredient Order**

When tacos are prepared within the home, individual ingredients shall be placed from the bottom to the top of the taco in accordance with the Vertical Taco Placement Chart. Any undesired ingredient may be omitted in the preparation of the taco. Regardless of taste, it is strictly forbidden to place a lower priority taco item above a higher priority taco item. Example: placing ground beef above lettuce.

A. Vertical Taco Placement Chart

Top of the taco	sour cream
Seventh Item	salsa, or other liquid sauce
Sixth Item	cheese
Fifth Item	black olives
Fourth Item	tomatoes
Third Item	lettuce
Second Item	any refried bean item
Bottom of the taco	meat, or meat substitute

B. Additional taco ingredients not on this list may be placed in any vertical position of the taco. However, no item shall be placed below the meat or above the sour cream.

C. Any deviation from BOR 5-4 clearly demonstrates the lack of good taste and respect for one's food.

   1. Respect your food.

BOR 5-5 | Peanut Butter and Jelly Thickness

The total combined thickness of peanut butter and jelly on a peanut butter and jelly sandwich shall not exceed 5/8 inch. The federally mandated thickness requirement has changed numerous times due to Congress's attempt to find a balance between sandwich satisfaction and spill prevention. Special interest groups and lobbyists currently work diligently on both sides of the political spectrum to increase or decrease the maximum allowable thickness of peanut butter and jelly sandwiches. A combined total of forty-seven million dollars is spent annually promoting the case to adjust the maximum allowable thickness. Most Americans patiently await the end of the twenty-first century PB&J controversy, which will allow both the Republican and Democratic parties to address more urgent American issues, such as health care, taxes and the national debt.

BOR 5-6 | The Cereal Prize

Cereal boxes should remain sealed until ready for use. Cereal boxes containing prizes may not be manipulated or searched to prematurely reveal or obtain the enclosed prize. Cereal should be poured evenly, randomizing the pour in which the prize is revealed. Anyone who observes another individual, of any age, prematurely or illegally obtaining a cereal box prize has a moral obligation to confiscate the item. Confiscated cereal box

BOR 5-6. Cereal boxes containing prizes may not be manipulated or searched to prematurely reveal or obtain the enclosed prize.

prize items shall be given to the youngest person residing in the home.

A. If the youngest individual residing in the home illegally obtains a cereal box prize, the prize shall be presented to a parent or guardian to be retained and given with the child's high school graduation gift.

BOR 5-7 | Chewing Gum

Research indicates that chewing gum reduces stress, provides satisfaction and may reduce cavities (if the gum is sugar-free). A supply of gum shall be kept at home, in automobiles and in purses (if applicable). When enjoyed, gum should be shared readily with others. When selecting a piece of gum within a pack to be chewed, care should be taken to select pieces in the center of the pack. Successive pieces shall be chosen from the center, outward, with the final two pieces to be the outer two pieces within the pack of gum.

A. Chewing gum is forbidden at work, school, church and all formal gatherings where public speaking may occur.

B. Teeth shall never be visible while chewing gum.

C. Except in the case of blowing bubbles, care should be taken to ensure that gum-chewing noise is not audible from a distance of more than 3 feet.

D. Gum shall be properly discarded when no longer in use.

   1. If an individual is observed illegally discarding gum, the used gum shall be sanitarily collected and placed in an envelope. This envelope shall be anonymously sent to the violator with the words "RETURNED TO SENDER" written as the return address.

BOR 5-8   The Drinking and Disposal of Milk

Milk is a crucial part of any individual's diet. Vitamins A, D, E and K are found in both grades of milk. Grade A milk is distributed for human consumption and Grade B milk is milk distributed for indirect consumption in the manufacture of dairy products such as cheese and sour cream. The advantages of drinking at least 1 cup of milk daily include increased stamina, dental health and the reduction of bone loss. Medical studies have indicated a link between the consumption of milk and the reduced risk of hypertension, obesity and heart disease.

A. Milk cartons must be discarded immediately after determining the milk has soured.

B. Milk may not be consumed directly from the carton in the presence of others.

C. Milk shall only be consumed in a glass or paper drinking receptacle except as outlined in BOR 9-5 B3.

D. After a milk carton is emptied, it shall be promptly discarded or recycled. Placing an empty milk carton back in the refrigerator may irritate other individuals seeking a milk beverage or a milk complement to other food items such as cereal or oatmeal. Careless empty carton placement sparks anger within the home and may trigger unnecessary unpleasantness.

   1. Milk cartons containing less than two ounces of milk are considered empty. The remaining milk shall be either consumed or discarded.

E. Lactose intolerant individuals should work to overcome their personal food discrimination issues. All foods should be judged equally despite negative dairy stereotypes, outward food appearances and personal food allergies.

BOR 5-9 | Salting Food

Salt is a natural mineral composed of mostly sodium chloride. It is essential in all diets but is unhealthy and even deadly in large quantities. Overconsumption contributes to numerous health problems including high blood pressure. Salt is the most commonly used spice in the preparation of food, and it is manufactured in three varieties: table salt, unrefined salt and iodized salt.

A. Prepared food shall not be salted before tasting.

B. Care should be taken in the purchase of salt and pepper shakers to ensure they accurately reflect the style and

BOR 5-9. Prepared food shall not be salted before tasting.

personality of the individuals living in the home
(see BOR 9-10).

   1. Salt and pepper shakers may not be given as gifts unless
      specifically requested in a registry.

C. Salt shakers may only be displayed on kitchen tables and
   stoves (see BOR 9-8 B).

D. The custom of tossing salt over one's shoulder for luck may
   not be practiced indoors unless the individual who takes this
   action subsequently cleans the floor.

BOR 5-10 | Pizza: Baked at Home or Delivered

Everybody likes pizza. Pizza is an inexpensive option for the
family dinner. Although high in fat, salt and calories, most

pizzas contain all four food groups. Pizza should always be served with at least one other food item. Suggested side dishes served with pizza include bread sticks, salad and pasta.

A. To ensure a crispy crust, home-prepared pizza shall always be baked directly on the center oven rack. The food preparation specialist (see BOR 9-11 A) or designee shall be responsible for cleanup after the oven cools, if necessary.

B. The use of coupons is encouraged when ordering home-delivered pizza.

1. Coupons not requested after the pizza transaction has been completed may be retained for future use. Drivers returning to the home to request pizza coupons not collected shall be turned away.

| BOR 5-11 | **Ice-Enhanced Beverages**

The four basic types of ice are cubed, cracked, shaved and block. Most Americans prefer beverages enhanced with ice. Larger ice cubes keep drinks cooler longer and reduce the water dilution of the beverage. Ice should always be prepared with the purest and cleanest water available. Stored ice should be replaced with new cubes regularly to reduce the absorption of odors from other stored foods.

A. Individuals removing ice from ice cube trays have a moral and ethical obligation to refill the tray whenever two cubes or fewer remain in the tray. Beverages are often needlessly consumed without thermal enhancement due to the careless actions of others.

B. Immediately after discovering the nonavailability of ice at a restaurant community soft drink receptacle, management or wait staff shall be notified. Patrons are required to wait by the ice machine for an appropriate time, generally five minutes or less, to ensure the ice replenishment request is honored.

C. The use of ice is authorized for all beverages except milk. Milk shall always be consumed refrigerated, but without ice, in a glass or paper drinking receptacle (see BOR 9-5 A1).

D. Ice should never be chewed in the close proximity of others.

   NOTE: The practice of inflicting torture by chewing ice near a blindfolded prisoner's ear was discontinued in the late twentieth century.

BOR 5-12 | Resealing Loaves of Bread

Bread, often considered a biblical food, is a staple food item in many homes. The baking of bread predates modern history. Traditional breads are baked either leavened or unleavened. Leavening is the process of adding a gas-producing substance to dough, such as yeast or baking soda, which produces fluffier and softer bread. Common types of American bread include white, wheat, whole grain, rye and sourdough.

A. After any number of slices of bread are removed from a sealed loaf, bread bags shall be resealed with a twist tie or the flat plastic chip to prevent air from entering. Countless numbers of otherwise great lunches are needlessly spoiled by stale bread.

NOTE: Most loving parents teach their kids about love, a good work ethic and manners, but fail to teach their children—the leaders of tomorrow—about proper bread loaf containment.

B. When bread sealant devices are not available, the plastic bread wrapper shall be twisted a minimum of three times and folded under the loaf to prevent spoilage.

| BOR 5-13 | **Consuming Dessert** |

Dessert is the final course consumed at the completion of a meal. Often a sweet food, dessert may consist of any food item including fruit. Common desserts include ice cream, cake and pudding. Desserts, when enjoyed, should always be savored and consumed more slowly than the rest of the meal.

BOR 5-12. When bread sealant devices are not available, the plastic bread wrapper shall be twisted a minimum of three times and folded under to prevent spoilage.

A. Dessert dishes should not be visible during the regular meal when dining with children.

B. The dinner entrée must be consumed by all members of a dining party before dessert is served.

   1. Hiding main course food items or feeding dinner food to pets immediately disqualifies an individual from dessert.

C. Dieting individuals may occasionally consume dessert before the meal to reduce the total caloric intake. This practice is allowable although discouraged.

BOR 5-14 | The Toothpick

The toothpick is a small stick of wood used to remove food debris from the teeth. Few things in life are more aggravating than having food stuck between one's teeth. Toothpicks are authorized only if food removal cannot be accomplished using the tongue or suction.

A. Facing other individuals is prohibited while using a toothpick.

B. Flinging, or the intentional propelling of food from the mouth while using a toothpick, is prohibited.

C. Toothpick usage and oral cleansing are prohibited in the presence of others at Class A and B restaurants (see BOR 4-1).

D. Toothpicks are not articles of clothing and may not be worn between the teeth.

BOR 5-15 | Reserving Leftovers

Whenever possible, leftovers should be divided into individual servings before storing in the refrigerator. All leftovers should be consumed or discarded within seven days. Individuals desiring specific leftovers shall leave clearly visible written reservation information. This may be accomplished by placing a note on a dish, annotating initials using a marker or other means.

A. The penalty for not consuming reserved leftovers within seven days is the forfeiture of leftover reservation rights for thirty days.

B. The following three penalties apply when one consumes another individual's reserved leftovers:

1. A public apology
2. A five dollar fine paid to the individual who incurred the loss
3. Forfeiture of leftover reservation rights for thirty days

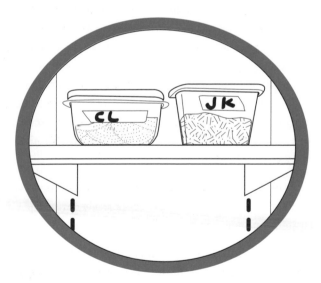

BOR 5-15. Individuals desiring specific leftovers shall leave clearly visible written reservation information.

6

HABITS AND MANNERS

BOR 6-1	**Proper Yawning Protocol**

Yawning is the act of simultaneously inhaling air and stretching the eardrums. Yawning is almost always accompanied with the extension of the arms. While experiencing a yawn, talking is forbidden from the moment an individual is aware that a yawn is initially occurring until one second after the completion of the yawn. Speaking during a yawn completely exposes the mouth and all that it may contain. Additionally, words spoken while yawning may be misinterpreted with potential dire consequences. Individuals who have spoken the words *sax* and *ship* while yawning know this all too well.

A. Only the yawning individual is required to cease conversation during a yawn. Others may speak freely during the entire duration of the yawn.

B. It is well recognized that yawning initiates a chain reaction of yawns by others. Therefore, the mouth shall be completely covered during a yawn and the head shall be tilted slightly away from others.

BOR 6-2 | Acknowledgment of a Sneeze

While generally harmless to others, sneezes may spread infectious diseases by propelling air, water droplets and germs at speeds exceeding ten miles per hour. Sneezing is generally triggered by subjection to foreign airborne particles or exposure to bright light. After it is determined that a sneeze is imminent, the sneeze should be completely executed. No attempt may be made to suppress a sneeze, regardless of the social situation. If time allows, one or two hands should be placed over the mouth to reduce the spread of germs.

A. Individuals with a known or suspected illness are encouraged to sneeze into their sleeve to prevent the spread of germs.

B. After a sneeze has been executed, all individuals within listening distance of the sneeze have the initial requirement to render a sneeze response phrase, such as "God Bless You."

C. Only one sneeze response is required, but additional sneeze responses may be offered by anyone in the audible proximity of the sneeze. The BOR 6-2 D Sneeze Acknowledgment Priority List shall be used to determine the individual with the primary responsibility for issuing the sneeze response. Individuals must wait two seconds to respond to a sneeze if a higher priority responder is in the immediate proximity of the sneezer.

D. Sneeze Acknowledgment Priority List

  1. The spouse or significant other of the sneezer
  2. Family members of the sneezer
  3. Friends of the sneezer
  4. Others in the audible proximity of the sneeze

BOR 6-2. Individuals with a known or suspected illness are encouraged to sneeze into their sleeve to prevent the spread of germs.

E. After hearing a sneeze response, the sneezer will reply with a gracious "Thank you," or similar reply. This action will be accomplished within five seconds after receiving a sneeze response.

F. In the case of successive sneezes, only the first two sneezes require a sneeze response. Successive sneezes require no additional action.

BOR 6-3 | Voluntary and Involuntary Coughing

The cough is a natural bodily reflex conducted to clear the breathing passage of irritants, foreign objects and secretions. Coughing can occur voluntarily and involuntarily. Both open- and closed-mouth coughs shall be executed with a single hand covering the entire mouth. Voluntary coughing is only allowable for the purpose of clearing one's throat.

A. Coughing for the purpose of gaining another's attention is considered vulgar and is therefore prohibited.

B. The reason for coughing more than three times in succession shall be disclosed to others, if known.

PHRASEOLOGY EXAMPLE: *"Excuse me, Carl. I'm allergic to cats. Why do you have five cats anyway?"*

BOR 6-4 | Acceptable Farting

Farting is the expulsion of gasses that are a by-product of digestion. The occurrence of this occasionally involuntary event increases significantly when foods such as beans, garlic and onions are consumed. Farting should always be executed appropriately and is generally discouraged in most social situations.

A. Farting noise shall always be limited to the extent possible.

B. Upon the receipt of a remark detailing the disgust of fart odor, a farter must offer an apologetic response, such as "Excuse me."

C. The practice of smiling and waving above one's middle section after farting is forbidden. Such practices encourage voluntary farting.

D. Farting is allowable without restriction whenever:

1. A farter is alone.

2. A male farter is among a group of other males and no females are present.

3. A farter is ill, bedridden or hospitalized.

4. A farter is attending any public event with one hundred or more individuals in attendance, and sufficient ambient noise exists to mask the farting noise and source.

E. Accusing another adult of farting is only permitted in the case of BOR 6-4 D2.

F. Farts consist primarily of nitrogen and carbon dioxide but also contain the flammable gases hydrogen and methane. The childish prank of "lighting one's fart" is considered extremely dangerous and is strongly discouraged.

BOR 6-5 | Burping in Public

Burping, also known as *belching* and *eructation,* typically occurs when gas is released from the stomach and esophagus through the mouth. Burping is often caused by the swallowing of air or by the consumption of carbonated beverages such as beer, champagne or other drinks containing carbon dioxide. Burping and belching are almost always associated with a specific sound and distinct odor. Burping noise should be minimalized whenever deemed socially inappropriate. The preferred writing hand shall be utilized to suppress expulsion. An immediate response, such as "Excuse me," should be expressed after the completion of the burp or belch.

BOR 6-6 | Notifying Individuals With Bad Breath

Halitosis is defined as a noticeable breath odor while exhaling. Bad breath usually originates from the mouth itself. Eating pungent foods such as garlic and onions increases the frequency and intensity of halitosis. Bad breath is typically most persistent in the morning, due to the inactivity of the mouth at night. Smoking and alcohol also contribute to bad breath. Proper hygiene, such as regular brushing and gargling with mouthwash, will reduce or eliminate the condition. Another method of reducing breath odor is the cleansing of the tongue, the most common location of bacteria in the mouth.

A. It is a civic responsibility to politely inform individuals with breath odor. Informing individuals with bad breath should be accomplished discreetly, ensuring the conversation is not overheard.

B. Brief, polite statements should be used to inform those with bad breath.

   PHRASEOLOGY EXAMPLE: *"You might want to brush your teeth."*

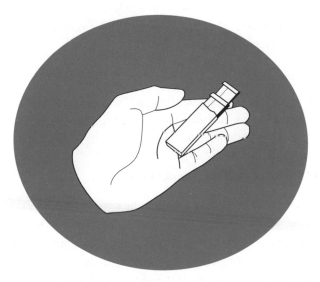

BOR 6-6. In lieu of notifying an individual of halitosis, the offering of a breath mint or gum adequately satisfies rule 6-6 A.

C. In lieu of notifying an individual of halitosis, the offering of a breath mint or gum adequately satisfies BOR 6-6 A.

D. After an individual is notified of bad breath, the noxious offender shall immediately excuse himself to remedy the oral situation by brushing, gargling or other means.

BOR 6-7 | Popping Pimples

Inexpensive modern acne medications have significantly reduced the severity of acne. Thorough facial cleansing reduces the appearance of pimples, specifically in young adults. The popping of pimples may worsen the condition, although such action is authorized if whiteheads or blackheads are visible.

A. Pimple popping shall always be conducted in private. Pimple poppers shall place themselves between 12 and 24 inches from a mirror.

B. Mirrors and countertops shall be wiped clean as necessary.

   1. Individuals caught not cleaning "pimple spray" shall be assigned a penalty appropriate to a teenager regardless of the age of the violator.

BOR 6-8 | The Habit of Smoking

Smoking is the practice of inhaling the smoke of burning tobacco. The addictive drug nicotine is absorbed into the lungs. Modern studies have proven that smoking causes lung cancer, heart attacks and birth defects. Smoking is unquestionably an unhealthy habit. New laws continue to make the practice more restrictive, resulting in cleaner air for everyone. The following

BOR 6-8. For luck, the first cigarette smoked in a pack will be the third from the left in the front row.

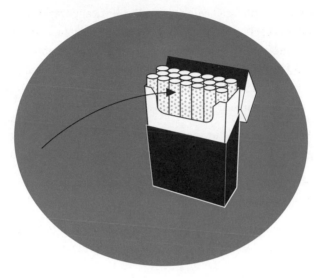

procedures are mandatory in addition to applicable state and federal laws:

A. Smoking in the designated smoking section of a restaurant is only permitted when all individuals within a group are known smokers.

B. The practice of smacking a fresh pack of cigarettes on the wrist for the purpose of forcing the tobacco toward the filter is allowable, yet discouraged.

   1. This practice is forbidden when it would cause a distraction in an inappropriate environment, such as a movie theater or college classroom.

C. For luck, the first cigarette smoked in a pack will be the third from the left in the front row.

BOR 6-9 | Elevator Etiquette

Elevators are mounted cars designed to vertically transport groups of people from one floor to another. Individuals should calmly and politely enter and exit elevators at all establishments. Elevator doors should be held open for all individuals entering or exiting the cab. The following elevator procedures are mandatory unless an emergency situation exists:

A. Healthy, non-handicapped adults are only authorized vertical transportation in an elevator when traveling two floors or more.

B. All exiting individuals shall be allowed to egress before elevator boarding may occur.

C. Children under the age of twelve may be allowed to "press the button" unless multiple children are present and feuding may occur.

D. Whenever polite conversation is initiated by another elevator occupant, acknowledgment is mandatory.

   1. Polite social conversational acknowledgment may be accomplished verbally or nonverbally with a smile, nod or other polite gestures.

E. Socially discouraged practices such as swearing and farting (see BOR 6-4) shall be avoided after the elevator doors have closed.

F. Singing or whistling along with elevator music is prohibited unless an individual is alone.

BOR 6-10 | Holding the Door

All men shall open the door for any female attempting entry or exit of any establishment. Chivalry is not dead, and the requirement to hold a door open for a woman is not gone. The number of "Thank You" and "You're Welcome" responses required to be spoken depend on the number of women entering or exiting an establishment.

A. One man opens door for one woman: "Thank You" response is required by the woman, and "You're Welcome" response is required by the man.

B. One man opens door for two women: "Thank You" response is required by both Women. "You're Welcome" response is required by the man if a "Thank You" is received.

C. One man opens door for three or more women: "Thank You" response is required by the first and last woman and optional for the other women. "You're Welcome" response is required by the man if a "Thank You" is received.

BOR 6-11 | Remembering Names

Every effort shall be made to remember a person's name after he or she has been introduced. Remembering names dramatically improves the way in which one is perceived. Mnemonic devices may be used to accomplish this task. Word association assists in the ability to rapidly recall an individual's name. For example, associating a newly introduced man named Don with the comedian Don Knotts will help to remember his name.

A. Adult individuals not yet introduced shall be addressed as "Sir" or "Ma'am."

B. Both male and female individuals previously introduced, but whose names have been forgotten, shall be addressed as "Guy," "Gal" or "Steve."

BOR 6-12 | Addressing Grandparents

Grandparents are addressed with a variety of affectionate names such as Grammy, Granny and Grandpappy. Most names are permissible, but the individual grandparent has the sole authorization in title selection. Individual grandparent name selection should be accomplished shortly after the birth of the first grandchild.

A. If more than one grandparent selects the same title, authorization for a specific title is granted to the grandparent who selects the title first. Other grandparents shall select another title.

B. Titles may not contain vulgarity or other words inappropriate when spoken in public.

C. Multiple titles are prohibited. For example, an individual grandparent cannot be Mammy to one grandchild and Grandma to another.

D. Occasional title changes are permitted provided all grandchildren are promptly notified of the change.

BOR 6-13 | Celebrating Birthdays

Birthdays shall be acknowledged by the family and friends of all individuals. Acknowledgment varies widely from simply stating "Happy Birthday" to elaborate parties based on the age, sex and desires of the celebrating person. The minimum "Happy Birthday" salutation must be accomplished by all immediate family members and close friends on or before the actual birthday. The birthday salutation may be offered via telephone, mail, in person or other means.

A. Individuals born on any nationally recognized holiday may elect to celebrate their birthday up to one week before or after their actual day of birth. For example, a man born on the Fourth of July may celebrate his birthday on July 10th.

B. Shortly after the birth of a child, parents should select a significant event to associate with the birthday of the child. Parents of a child born on October 9th, for example, may designate John Lennon's birthday as the significant event and incorporate that theme into future birthdays. In this case, a Beatles song may be sung to the child in lieu of "Happy Birthday."

C. Cake, candles and party favors of any variety are required elements at any birthday party for an individual age seventeen or younger.

BOR 6-13. Birthday cards received from immediate family members and close friends must be retained and displayed within the home for at least seven days.

D. Disclosing the age of a woman between the ages of thirty and sixty-five is forbidden without pervious verbal consent (see BOR 4-4 B).

E. Birthday cards received from immediate family members and close friends must be retained and displayed within the home for at least seven days.

BOR 6-14 | Mispronouncing Words

Every effort should be made to ensure the English language is spoken correctly. Everyone should strive to continually increase and improve personal vocabulary. Mispronouncing words negatively impacts the way in which one is perceived. Commonly mispronounced words include "library," "realtor" and "federal."

A. Always conduct the correction of someone's grammar politely and discreetly.

PHRASEOLOGY EXAMPLE: *"Hey Carla, it's pronounced library."*

B. Regional citizens may defend a mispronunciation by using a phrase such as, "We don't say it that way around here." In such cases, a BOR D-1 Discrepancy Form may be issued for violating BOR 1-2 A and BOR 6-14.

BOR 6-15 | Table Manners

Table manners are the rules of etiquette when consuming food in the presence of one or more individuals. At least one meal per day should be consumed at the dinner table with all members of the home (see BOR 9-12). A verbal blessing should be accomplished prior to the beginning of each meal. Verbal blessings may be a religious prayer or a simple verbal phrase to give thanks.

A. Hands must be washed prior to the consumption of food.

B. Children sixteen and under shall ask to be excused before leaving the table. Individuals seventeen and older shall verbally and politely excuse themselves before leaving the table.

C. No food may be consumed before all members of a dining party have been seated and served.

   1. Nonseated individuals may allow a meal to begin in their absence for a variety of acceptable reasons.

D. Cell phone usage is prohibited at the dinner table. Reading is permissible only at breakfast.

E. Every individual at the table is responsible for moving dishes and silverware to the dishwasher or the kitchen sink after the completion of the meal.

F. All diners shall express gratitude to the food preparation specialist (see BOR 9-11 A) prior to the completion of the meal.

   1. An honest and polite response shall be offered when the food preparation specialist (see BOR 9-11 A) asks an opinion concerning the quality of the food. A verbal compliment shall be included with every complaint about the food.

      PHRASEOLOGY EXAMPLE: *"The meat loaf was a little dry, but the bread pudding was excellent"* is favorable over *"What? You mean that was meat loaf? I thought that was the roadkill I ran over with the Buick."*

BOR 6-16 | Social Timeliness

Care should be taken to ensure timeliness at social functions relative to the importance of the event and the timeliness factor of an individual. The personal timeliness factor is expressed as a two-digit alphanumeric expression comprised of one letter and one number, such as A-2. The timeliness factor number is determined using the BOR 6-16 B Personal Timeliness Factor Chart.

A. An individual's timeliness factor number shall be annotated on an individual's state-issued driver's license using a marker or grease pencil.

B. Personal Timeliness Factor Chart

GENERAL TIMELINESS		CONSISTENCY								
		1	2	3	4	5	6	7	8	9
		very consistent ·················> sporadically								
A	arrive ten to fifteen minutes early (or more)									
B	arrive on time									
C	arrive on time or slightly late									
D	arrive ten to fifteen minutes late (or more)									

For example, an individual who always arrives on time for social events would be defined as "B-1."

C. Individuals who arrive late at social functions may be excused if they provide proof on a driver's license of a C 1-5 or D 1-5 personal timeliness factor number.

BOR 6-16. An individual's timeliness factor number shall be annotated on an individual's state-issued driver's license using a marker or grease pencil.

1. Recent studies have proven that social tardiness is both a physical and mental disability. Habitually tardy individuals may not be ridiculed.

2. The Timeliness Disabled Americans Task Force (TDATF) actively works to include timeliness disabled Americans as a protected class in anti-discrimination laws. However, due to the procrastinative nature of most members of the TDATF, little action or change is expected for several decades.

THE HOME

BOR 7-1 | **Sixty-Second Sofa Seat Reservation**

An individual leaving his or her spot on the sofa with the intention of returning to the same position may initiate a sixty-second sofa seat reservation. Reservations shall be accomplished verbally. After a sofa seat reservation has been initiated, a sixty-second countdown begins. No person may occupy any portion of the sofa occupied by the exiting individual during the countdown period. The exiting individual may reclaim the sofa position at any time during the countdown. After the sixty-second countdown period has expired, the empty spot on the sofa may be occupied by any individual on a first come, first served basis.

PHRASEOLOGY EXAMPLE: *"Save my seat, Sam."*

BOR 7-2 | **Authorized Use of Wind Chimes**

The popularity of wind chimes can be traced back to the American Indian wind bells. Often thought to bring good luck, the sound created from wind chimes can be heard for hundreds of feet. This sound can be relaxing and create a sense of peace in some individuals. However, houseguests and neighbors may find the sound offensive, especially at night.

A. Wind chimes are authorized for urban residents after verbal or written permission is obtained from all neighboring residents within aural distance.

   1. Verbal approval shall be accomplished with at least one witness.

   2. Written approval shall be retained and available for immediate retrieval upon request.

      PHRASEOLOGY EXAMPLE: *I, [Andy Mason], authorize neighbor [Anne Jezek] to display outdoor wind chimes without restriction. I formally release [Anne Jezek] from all liability of sleep loss, vertigo or other medical and mental conditions that may occur as a direct result of the display of outdoor wind chimes.*

B. Wind chimes are authorized for rural residents without restriction.

C. Houseguests spending the night shall be immediately notified of the existence of wind chimes.

   PHRASEOLOGY EXAMPLE: *"Hey Steve, it's really great to see you, but before you decide to spend the night, I'm required to let you know we have wind chimes. I can find alternate accommodations for you, if necessary."*

D. Information found on "wind chime tracker" websites, which disclose the names and addresses of wind chime owners, may not be used to commit acts of arson, burglary or theft.

BOR 7-3 | Displaying Wall Art

Decorative items displayed on walls in the home generally evoke a warm and inviting atmosphere. However, an excessive display of photographs and personal items significantly negates this effect. There is no limit to the number of photos that may be displayed, but personal items may not comprise more than one-half of the total items displayed on home walls.

A. Decorative wall art may be given as gifts. However, it is the sole discretion of the homeowner to display gifted items.

B. Individuals will be politely and tactfully advised if a decorative wall art gift is undesired or unwanted.

   PHRASEOLOGY EXAMPLE: *"Wow Steve, you really shouldn't have! I really like the neon velvet Elvis lithograph, but my wife says it doesn't go with our leather furniture."*

BOR 7-4 | Placing Good Luck Door Coins

For the purpose of enhancing good luck, at least one coin shall be placed above the door trim of the main entryway of every home. The resident of the home, regardless of ownership, shall accomplish this task. Coins may be any denomination of legal currency for the geographical location of the home. This action shall be completed within 72 hours of establishing residence in a home. Coins left by previous residents shall be left in place but may be examined for brief periods, provided they are replaced. Whenever coins from previous residents prevent the placement of additional coins, new coins shall be placed above the trim of any other door in the home.

BOR 7-4. For the purpose of enhancing good luck, at least one coin shall be placed above the door trim of the main entryway of every home.

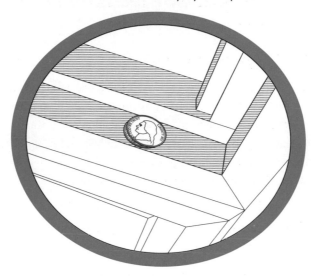

BOR 7-5 | Replacing Smoke Detector Batteries

Smoke detectors save lives. All smoke detectors should be kept in proper working order, and batteries should be replaced as needed. A commonly accepted practice suggests battery replacement should be accomplished on the day of daylight savings time and the day reverting back to standard time each year. This recommended practice is optional. However, after the low battery chirp from a smoke alarm is first heard, the batteries shall be immediately replaced for two very distinct but equally important reasons:

A. The safety of all individuals residing in the home is jeopardized with an improperly operating smoke detector.

B. The risk of criminal insanity due to the audible low battery chirp heard at regular intervals threatens everyone in the household.

BOR 7-6   Washing Care Tags

Sheets, blankets, comforters and quilts shall be arranged on beds with the washing care tag positioned at the foot of the bed. Tags placed at the head of the bed (pillow side) hinder restful sleep by distracting individuals in bed. Additionally, sleeping with the tag at the head of the bed is generally seen as an act of dishonor in most industrialized nations.

A. When allowable by law, tags may be removed. After removal of tag, sheets and other mattress complements may be placed in any position on the bed.

B. Instilling fear in individuals who remove washing care tags is authorized only between siblings.

BOR 7-7   Displaying Outdoor Decorations

Outdoor holiday decorations may be displayed during the time which purchase is authorized, as outlined in BOR 3-9 A. Indoor holiday decorations must be removed within seven days after the end of the holiday. Outdoor decorations may be displayed slightly longer, but in no event shall these items be displayed after January 31st of the following year.

A. Outdoor seasonal holiday lights, when displayed, shall be operated from dusk until three hours after sunset. Automatic electric timers may be utilized to accomplish this task.

BOR 7-7. Despite urban legends and myths, there is no mandate for Texas residents to display an outdoor star.

B. Seasonal outdoor display competitions between neighbors are authorized. However, spite decorating is strictly prohibited. Good taste and sound judgment should be exercised when considering individual displays.

  1. Spite decorating is defined as the practice of excessively decorating for the sole purpose of impressing or belittling neighbors.

C. Nearly 94 percent of homes in the state of Texas display a star on the exterior of the home. Despite urban legends and myths, there is no mandate for Texas residents to display an outdoor star.

BOR 7-8 | Operating Washers and Dryers

High-efficiency washers and dryers substantially reduce operating costs and should be considered when purchasing new appliances. Washers and dryers should be operated in a separate laundry room of the home with the door closed when practical. Discount detergents, fabric softeners and dryer sheets may be routinely used only if a significant savings results from the purchase of discount products.

A. The individual who starts a washer cycle is responsible for ensuring the dryer cycle is started within one hour after washing is completed. If ample time is not allotted to complete both the washer and dryer cycle, a load of laundry may not be started.

B. Dryer lint shall be removed and discarded immediately after removing clothing.

C. Clothing not removed from dryers within one hour after a dryer cycle completes shall be either pressed or refluffed in the dryer.

D. Washing "white" and "color" clothing together in the same load is prohibited in the presence of women or anyone else who knows better.

BOR 7-9 | Proper Closet Organization

Household closets should be kept neat and orderly. Proper organization enhances productivity and reduces stress. Only articles of clothing intended to be worn within one year are authorized to stay in the closet. Individuals sharing closets must equitably divide rack and shelf space based on personal clothing inventories (see BOR 10-2).

A. Strict divisions of closet space shall be established and maintained. Typically for married couples, one-third of closet space is designated for the man and two-thirds for the woman.

B. Closet floors shall be cleaned at the same frequency as bedroom floors.

C. The marking of walls measuring and annotating the height progression of children shall take place only on closet walls. Wall height measurement markings shall never be removed regardless of home ownership.

   1. The repainting of walls containing height measurement markings is authorized, but height positions must be annotated and accurately rewritten after painting.

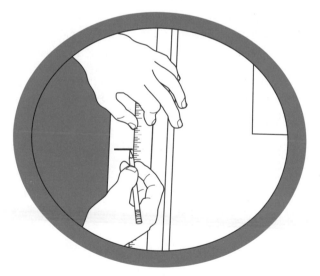

BOR 7-9. Prior to repainting walls containing height measurement markings, height positions must be annotated.

BOR 7-10 | Hiding Spare Keys

Maintaining spare keys reduces the likelihood of being locked out of a home. The inability to enter a household may create a significant safety risk. In addition, locksmith fees are generally quite expensive. Two spare keys shall be made for the front door of every home.

A. The first spare key shall be hidden in the front yard or other location within 100 feet of the front door. This key shall not be visible from any angle. The location of the first spare key shall be clearly communicated to all residents of the home.

   1. Spare keys shall never be hidden under doormats (see BOR 7-13).

B. The second spare key shall be maintained by a relative, friend or neighbor who resides within 1 mile of the home. This individual shall be designated as the "key holder." The identity, address and phone number of the key holder shall be clearly communicated to all individuals residing in the home.

   1. Designating key holder services to an individual does not specifically require that key holder services be reciprocally provided, although this practice is encouraged.

   2. Key holders may never disclose the identity of the owners of the keys they maintain.

   3. Key owners and key holders shall verbally verify spare keys are maintained at least once each year.

BOR 7-11 | Dealing With Yard Parkers

The primary purpose of a garage is to store and protect automobiles, motorcycles and bicycles. Vehicles may not be routinely parked in driveways nor in the street if a stall is open in the garage. Garages shall be considered secondary storage areas. Miscellaneous household items shall not be stored in garages if space is available in primary storage areas such as attics, closets and sheds. Every effort shall be made to ensure ample parking space exists in garages. Boxes containing nonseasonal items stored in garages shall be considered unnecessary and excessive if boxes have not been opened in the previous year. Excessive items shall be discarded as appropriate.

A. Individuals who routinely park vehicles outside of garages, when garage space is available, shall be identified as "yard parkers." Yard parkers may be excluded from all neighborhood events such as parties, meetings and community garage sales until they use the garage to capacity.

BOR 7-11. Miscellaneous household items shall not be stored in garages if space is available in primary storage areas such as attics, closets and sheds. Every effort shall be made to ensure ample parking space exists in garages.

B. Individuals possessing more vehicles than garage capacity allows will not be considered yard parkers.

C. Yard parkers may not be scorned, harassed or ridiculed unless violators physically park vehicles in the front yard.

BOR 7-12 | **Wearing Shoes in the Home**

Many American households prohibit the wearing of shoes in the house to prevent dirt and mud from being tracked in the home. The decision of whether or not to wear shoes within the home shall be made collectively by all adult residents. The owner of a "no shoes" home shall ensure a shoe receptacle is placed in close proximity to the front door. The purpose of the placement of a shoe receptacle is to indicate the designation of a "no shoes" home.

A. House slippers worn outside the home are considered shoes and may not be worn in a "no shoes" designated home.

B. All shoe receptacles in a "n -shoes" home shall have at least one pair of house slippers intended for houseguests.

C. A commonly used expression is often recited at the door of a "no shoes" home: "When in Rome, do as the Romans do. When you are in my home, take off your shoes, you filthy pig. I know you weren't raised in a barn. In fact, I know your mother, and she would be furious if she saw you walking on my clean floors with those shoes. You know, I just mopped on Wednesday. I'm going to give your mom a quick call. And don't even think of moving from that spot. I'll tell her you said hi."

Proper doormat selection, placement and cleanliness significantly contribute to a positive first impression of an individual's home. Doormats should accurately reflect the style and theme of the home and may contain personalized text. One outdoor doormat shall be kept at each entrance of the home, and one indoor doormat shall be kept immediately inside the main entrance of the home.

A. The placement of an undecorated doormat containing only the word "Welcome" reflects a lack of creativity and is discouraged.

B. All doormats shall be cleaned at least monthly.

C. Spare keys shall never be hidden under doormats (see BOR 7-10).

BOR 7-14 | **Maintaining the Yard**

Yards should be well kept and maintained. The selection of decorative yard items should be tasteful and blend with the selected household decorative theme (see BOR 9-10). Watering early in the morning prevents evaporation and the growth of mold and fungus in the lawn. A total of 1 inch of water is to be applied to most lawns weekly. Fertilization should be accomplished in the spring and the fall.

A. Suburban residents shall mow lawns weekly or when grass height exceeds 4 inches, whichever occurs first. Rural residents shall mow lawns bimonthly or when grass height exceeds 5 inches, whichever occurs first.

B. The purchase and use of a riding lawn mower is prohibited for yards smaller than 50,000 square feet.

C. The authorization to borrow yard work equipment from neighbors is allowable up to three times per item per year. Borrowed equipment shall be cleaned and returned within 48 hours after use.

D. Decorative yard items may be placed in any configuration in front lawns with a maximum total limit of six items.

BOR 7-15 | Maximum Allowable Number of Pets

Over half of American households have at least one pet. The ownership of pets offers significant benefits including the reduction of blood pressure, reduced risk of depression and increased sense of purpose. The ownership of a pet should be considered a lifetime commitment for all needs including feeding, grooming and medical care. Pets offer unconditional love, and their ownership is encouraged.

A. A total maximum number of four pets may be kept in the home.

1. A single aquarium counts as one pet regardless of the number of fish.

B. A pet owner is solely responsible for the removal of pet fecal matter from the front lawn and all locations away from the home.

C. Under no circumstances may a pet consume food at the dinner table or any other location where family members dine.

D. The dressing of pets in clothing is discouraged. The dressing of pets in clothing that matches the owner's clothing in color, theme or style is strictly prohibited.

BOR 7-15. The dressing of pets in clothing that matches the owner's clothing in color, theme or style is strictly prohibited.

BOR 7-16 | Parties at Home

Occasional parties strengthen interpersonal relationships with co-workers, neighbors and friends. The invitation of next-door neighbors to parties that may continue past midnight is strongly recommended. The guest list for parties should be determined equitably by all adult members in the home.

A. The party host is responsible for providing food and drink specifically intended for parties. Leftover food does not constitute party food.

B. Standard party cups must always be red.

C. Mixed drinks at formal parties shall be served with drink umbrellas.

1. *Formal* is a relative term based on the standards of the host. For example, a formal party for college students would include any occasion in which beer pong, binge drinking and nudity were prohibited.

BOR 7-17 | Shoveling Snow

Homeowners are responsible for shoveling any driveways and sidewalks that exist on personal property. Every homeowner should do their part to ensure sidewalks and driveways are kept clear of snow and ice. Shoveling immediately after a snowstorm is often an easier task than shoveling later, after the snow melts and refreezes. Additionally, shoveling in stages can make a large job a lot easier.

A. Shoveling sidewalks shall be conducted by able-bodied homeowners after a snow depth of 4 inches or more is first observed or within 12 hours after snow has stopped falling.

B. Shoveled snow may not be piled onto sidewalks, the street or the lawns of neighbors.

C. Yellow snow, although possessing the color and consistency of a pineapple snow cone, should not be consumed.

8

BATHROOMS

| BOR 8-1 | Toilet Paper Selection and Placement |

Along with coal, lumber and oil, premium toilet paper is a natural resource and must be treated with respect. The wasteful practice of abusing toilet paper clogs toilets and rapidly diminishes household toilet paper supplies. Good judgment shall be exercised in the selection, placement and usage of toilet paper.

A. Only quilted, two-ply toilet paper may be used unless a personal financial hardship prevents the purchase of premium paper. The removal of all frivolous household expenses, such as health club membership and cable television, must be accomplished before nonpremium toilet paper is purchased. Even the thriftiest of individuals are encouraged to splurge monetarily in three specific areas:

1. Tipping those who prepare one's food
2. Tipping those who style one's hair
3. Premium toilet paper

BOR 8-1. Toilet paper shall be dispensed from the roll with new sheets advancing from the bottom of the roll.

B. Toilet paper sheets shall be dispensed five sheets or fewer with each tear. Additional dispensing in increments of five sheets or fewer is permissible as needed.

C. Toilet paper shall be dispensed from the roll with new sheets advancing from the bottom of the roll.

  1. Whenever an individual observes an incorrectly placed roll of toilet paper, the roll shall be removed and properly placed. In the case of a houseguest "righting" a toilet paper roll, the homeowner shall be politely notified.

     PHRASEOLOGY EXAMPLE: *"Hey Clifford, your toilet paper was on wrong!"*

D. A sufficient supply of toilet paper shall be maintained in every bathroom. The complete exhaustion of toilet paper will initiate a 12-hour countdown to replacement. The individual who becomes initially aware of the exhaustion has the primary responsibility of replenishment. This responsibility may only be designated if another individual may more expeditiously accomplish the task.

E. Care shall be taken to protect toilet paper from stray water, which may dampen the roll and reduce its effectiveness and absorbency.

F. Toilet sheets will be torn at the perforation from the right to the left.

G. Emergency toilet paper consists of any absorbent material that may be utilized after the discovery of the nonavailability of toilet paper. The selection of emergency toilet paper shall be determined based upon the availability of the following items, in order:

1. Facial tissues
2. Paper towels
3. Napkins
4. Newspapers
5. Magazines
6. BOR G-1 Utility Form (see BOR Appendix C)

BOR 8-2 | Locking the Bathroom Door

Spare skeleton bathroom keys should be kept in near proximity to bathroom doors. Often these keys consist of little more than a screwdriver or pen. Bathroom doors shall be closed or locked depending on the identity of individuals currently in the home. Door knocking is mandatory before entry whenever a household bathroom may be occupied.

A. Bathroom doors may be left ajar if an individual is alone or at home with only the spouse or cohabiting "significant other" currently at home.

B. Bathroom doors shall be closed but may be unlocked when only cohabiting family members are currently at home.

C. Bathroom doors shall be closed and locked in all other situations.

D. Bathroom doors may be optionally closed or locked by the occupant regardless of the social situation.

BOR 8-3 | The Use of Soap

Soap is a body cleansing agent that is usually sold in solid bars or in the form of a liquid. Body cleansing should always be conducted using soap. At least one bar of soap should be readily available at every sink and shower within the home. Hand washing is required after using the restroom.

A. The use of antibacterial soap is discouraged. Antibacterial soap promotes the growth of antibiotic-resistant bacteria and gradually weakens the body's natural immune system.

B. Liquid soap shall be available in all bathrooms shared by two or more people.

C. Bar soap is considered unusable after the width is reduced to a thickness of ¼ inch or less. Bar soap shall be discarded and replaced after the ¼-inch thickness is first observed.

D. Guests using restrooms at friends' and neighbors' homes are exempt from BOR 8-5 whenever soap, toilet paper or towels are not readily available.

BOR 8-4 | Dental Floss Guidelines

Modern dental floss consists of a thin nylon thread used to remove plaque and food lodged between the teeth. Dentists generally recommend flossing, as toothbrushes cannot effectively reach between the teeth. Used dental floss shall be discarded in an appropriate trash receptacle immediately after use. When a restroom trash receptacle cannot be found (see BOR 9-6), used floss should be carried to and disposed of in the nearest trash receptacle. Used floss should never be placed on bathroom counters. The reckless disposal of soiled floss promotes the spread of countless infectious diseases.

A. Flossing should be accomplished daily but shall be accomplished at least weekly.

B. Facing another individual while flossing is prohibited.

C. Food removed from teeth while flossing may never be consumed.

D. Alternate uses for dental floss include ribbon for wrapping presents, shoelaces and emergency guitar strings.

BOR 8-5 | Looking in a Friend's Medicine Cabinet

During a bathroom visit, it is strictly forbidden to open a friend's bathroom cabinet or closet door unless a genuine need exists. Allowable needs include, but are not limited to, missing towels, missing soap and toilet paper exhaustion. Many friendships have been needlessly ended by the innocent act of "sneaking a peek." Looking in a friend's medicine cabinet is a betrayal of trust.

BOR 8-6 | Towel Folding and Display

At least one bath towel and one hand towel intended for use should be displayed in every bathroom. Personalized towels, such as monogrammed hand towels, do not count toward the minimum number. Spare towels should be stored in an obvious bathroom location such as under the sink.

A. Bathroom towels shall never be rolled. All bathroom towels intended for use shall be displayed on towel rings, towel rods or folded in a convenient location.

B. Towels in actively utilized bathrooms shall be washed at least weekly.

C. The common American 2′ x 4′ towel shall be folded as follows: Top to bottom, top to bottom, and then a tri-fold from left to right. Adherence to this regulation is paramount. Numerous instances of vandalism have occurred after friends and neighbors illegally investigate linen closets (see BOR 8-5)

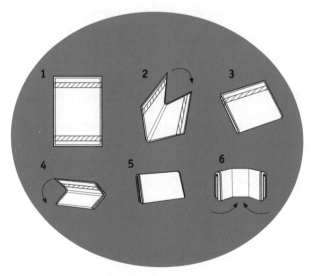

BOR 8-6. The common American 2 x 4-foot towel shall be folded as follows: Top to bottom, top to bottom, and then a tri-fold from left to right.

in bathrooms. Their disgust at the sight of improperly folded towels has sparked cruel and occasionally violent acts.

1. Temporary living arrangements or insufficient cabinet space permit alternative towel-folding options provided all household occupants agree.

BOR 8-7 | Recommended Facial Tissue Selection

Facial tissue is a high-quality, soft and absorbent paper intended for use on the face. Usually sold in boxes, facial tissue is generally used to cleanse the face after blowing your nose. Tissue selection should be a variety consisting of two or three plies.

A. A supply of tissues shall be kept in every bathroom and at least one other location in the home.

B. Facial tissue boxes must be displayed within four feet of toilets in all household bathrooms (see BOR 8-1 G).

BOR 8-8 | Cotton Swab Usage

Cotton swabs consist of a small rod of either plastic or paper with cotton wrapped around either or both ends. The cotton swab is the universally recognized and recommended method for ear wax removal. Eliminating ear wax improves hearing and reduces the unsightly appearance of wax in the ears.

A. Earwax removal with an FDA-approved cotton swab shall be accomplished at least once each week.

B. Weekly ear cleaning shall include at least two fresh swabs, one applied to each ear.

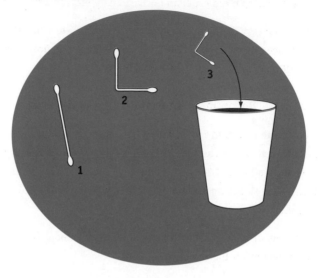

BOR 8-8. Immediately after use, cotton swabs shall be bent before discarding to prevent unintentional reuse.

C. Immediately after use, cotton swabs shall be bent before discarding to prevent unintentional reuse.

D. Couples considering divorce or separation due to spouses not listening should consider the purchase of quality cotton swabs for their partner as a surprise gift.

BOR 8-9 | Brushing Your Teeth

Proper oral hygiene not only protects the teeth but also helps prevent heart disease. Brushing teeth properly effectively fights against tooth loss, cavities and periodontal disease. Brushing teeth regularly helps ensure overall dental health. Teeth shall be thoroughly brushed each morning and before going to bed. Only soft-bristled American Dental Association (ADA) approved brushes may be used, as medium- and hard-bristle brushes irritate the gums.

A. The utilization of another individual's toothbrush is strictly forbidden.

B. All toothbrushes shall be placed in a holding receptacle, bristles up, when not in use. Any holding receptacle satisfies this requirement, provided the bristles of brushes do not touch countertops or other surfaces, including other brushes.

C. Teeth shall be brushed at least 10 inches from bathroom mirrors.

D. Whenever less than 50 percent of toothpaste remains in the tube, the brusher shall force as much toothpaste as possible to the front of the tube.

   1. Forcing toothpaste to the front of the tube may be accomplished by rolling the rear of the tube, sliding the tube across the edge of the bathroom countertop or other means.

BOR 8-10 | Shaving Protocol

Regular shaving helps ensure a clean cut and professional look. Shaving is strongly recommended on days in which work is conducted and optional on regular days off. Bathroom shaving areas shall be briefly wiped clean to remove stubble, shaving cream and stray water after shaving.

A. Disposable razors may never be stored in contact with toothbrushes.

B. Razor stubble may never be visible on bathroom countertops or bathtubs.

C. Shaving may never be conducted in automobiles. Fortunately, natural selection will gradually remove individuals from

BOR 8-10. Shaving may never be conducted in automobiles.

society who simultaneously shave, smoke and operate cell phones while driving (see BOR 11-8 D).

| BOR 8-11 | **Recommended Showering Schedule**

For the purpose of body cleansing, showering is generally the preferred method (see BOR 8-12). Showering most effectively cleanses the body by rinsing the body from the top down. While showering, individual body parts shall be cleansed from the head to the feet.

A. Showering shall be accomplished daily. To ensure maximum daily cleanliness, showers should be taken in the morning unless an evening shower will provide a specific operational advantage.

B. The entire body should be cleansed while showering. Both feet shall be picked up and washed. Soap and water running over the feet does meet the body-cleansing requirement.

C. All shampoo and conditioner containers must be properly resealed after use. Partially open containers and stray shower water cause the dilution of hair products.

1. It is unclear how many job interviews failed and dates were unsuccessful due solely to bad hair. Improperly sealed shampoo items have hindered countless careers and are a contributing factor in many failed relationships.

BOR 8-12 | **Optional Bathtub Bathing**

For the purpose of body cleansing, showering is generally the preferred method. Bathing is soothing and peaceful and is allowable for relaxation. However, bathtub bathing is an ineffective method for body cleansing, as much of the dirt and grime washed off the body is reabsorbed into the skin.

A. Whenever showering facilities are not available, bathtub bathing is authorized without restriction.

B. Bathtub bathing is authorized and socially acceptable for the ill, the elderly, the disabled and children eleven years of age and younger.

C. Bathtub toys, such as rubber ducks, are authorized for bathers of any age, provided they are properly stored after use.

BOR 8-13 | **The Use of Bathroom Scales**

Bathroom scales provide an excellent measure of diet progression and general health. Weight measuring scales, when owned,

BOR 8-13. The sophomoric prank of intentionally adjusting bathroom scales to reveal a heavier weight is strictly prohibited.

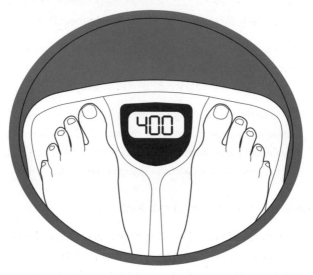

may be kept only in bathrooms. Only digital scales or scales with an adjustable zero point may be used. The zero point should be analyzed and adjusted, if necessary, before each use. The use of bathroom scales should be conducted immediately after showering or while wearing a minimal clothing.

A. Weight measurement may be conducted up to a maximum of twice daily.

B. The possession of "talking" scales or other novelty scales is prohibited.

C. The sophomoric prank of intentionally adjusting bathroom scales to reveal a heavier weight is strictly prohibited.

BOR 8-14 | Preparing a Guest Bathroom

A single restroom may be designated as the guest bathroom for houseguests staying longer than one day. Guest bathrooms will be thoroughly cleaned within 24 hours of the arrival of the houseguest. To the extent possible, guest bathrooms should not be used by residents whenever a guest is staying in the home.

A. In addition to everyday toiletries, guest bathrooms will be stocked with guest toiletries. Guest toiletries include, but are not limited to:

   1. Room deodorizer
   2. At least one candle
   3. Plunger
   4. Reading material collectively appropriate to all visiting houseguests

B. Visiting houseguests may not be charged more than $1 per guest per day for the use of a guest bathroom.

BOR 8-15 | Men's Public Restroom Rules

It is often necessary for males to use public restrooms with urinals placed in a row along a wall. This creates a shoulder to shoulder configuration of men, which is quite uncomfortable for most men. The following guidelines were established to reduce the perceived reduction of manhood while conducting a necessary bodily function:

A. Care should be taken to ensure the urinal or stall selected does not neighbor another man when occupancy allows.

B. Every effort shall be made to avoid eye contact with other individuals using the facility.

C. Vocal exchanges are forbidden.

   1. Conversation with other individuals must be abruptly halted after a man stands in position behind a urinal.

   2. Halted conversation may be promptly resumed after both men are no longer in position.

   3. Brief statements may be made in position if it is determined that omission will have a significant negative impact on anyone in the facility. For example, it is allowable to say, "I saw a rat in that urinal," while in position.

      a. Acknowledgment to necessary statements shall always be accomplished nonverbally. These acknowledgments are generally affirmative or negative nods and hand gestures.

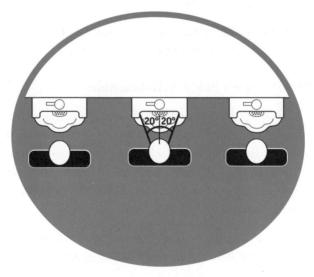

BOR 8-15. Head motion is restricted to 20° to the left or right of the centerline of the orientation of an individual while in position.

D. Head motion is restricted to 20° to the left or right of the centerline of the orientation of an individual while in position.

E. Loud moans and sighs of relief while in position are permissible when not directed at other individuals and when no comprehensible words can be discerned.

   1. This practice is generally considered vulgar and strongly discouraged.

BOR 8-16 | Women's Public Restroom Rules

The procedures for women's public restrooms differ considerably from male facilities and are significantly less restrictive. As women's visits to public restrooms are sometimes social visits, good manners and grace shall always be exercised to the extent possible. These guidelines were established to enhance communication, reduce long lines and streamline the effectiveness of an often chaotic process.

A. In the event of long bathroom wait lines, women should be conscientious of others. Women requiring the immediate use of facilities shall be given priority in line.

   1. Whenever bathroom facilities are overcrowded, and long lines are present, women shall utilize facilities as expeditiously as possible. Social interactions shall be conducted politely and promptly.

B. Any conversation conducted in public restrooms shall be considered confidential and falls under the Women's Code of Communication. Such information shall not be shared with others unless specific verbal approval has been obtained.

1. Any conversation falling under the Women's Code of Communication shall be abruptly terminated after any of the conversing women exit the restroom.

2. Loitering in public restrooms for the sole purpose of over-hearing information covered under the Women's Code of Communication is prohibited.

C. Inexpensive toiletries shall be willingly shared with any woman in need.

D. The existence of lavish accommodations in women's restrooms, such as recliners or hot towels, may never be discussed with men.

9

KITCHENS

BOR 9-1 | **Kitchen Clock Regulations**

One and only one wall clock shall be placed in the kitchen at the average eye level of all adult residents within a home. This requirement is mandatory regardless of the existence of additional digital time displays on appliances. Wall clocks may be placed on any wall of the kitchen but should be visible from any position in the room.

A. The primary kitchen wall clock shall be mechanical.

B. All kitchen appliance digital time displays shall be set to agree with a tolerance of +/- 10 seconds of each other and the primary wall clock.

   1. Clocks may be intentionally set fast or slow for various reasons, provided all clocks are coordinated accurately within the 10-second tolerance.

C. Decorative novelty clocks, such as a "dancing Mickey Mouse" are prohibited in the kitchen. Novelty clocks may be placed in any other room of the house.

BOR 9-1. One and only one wall clock shall be placed in the kitchen at the average eye level of all adult residents within a home.

BOR 9-2 | Organization of Cabinets and Drawers

To the extent possible, small kitchen items should be stored in kitchen cabinets and drawers. Small kitchen items should not be stored on countertops unless sufficient cabinet space does not exist or the items in question are routinely utilized. Except as required below, all household members must agree on the placement of small kitchen items.

A. Pots and pans shall be stored in the nearest cabinet to the kitchen stove.

B. Cloth protective items, such as pot holders, shall be stored in the nearest drawer to the kitchen stove.

C. General use silverware shall be placed in the drawer nearest to the kitchen sink.

D. Small miscellaneous kitchen items shall be stored in a designated junk drawer or holding receptacle on the kitchen counter.

E. Close friends and family members of homeowners forced to search for misplaced items are authorized to collect and hide all small kitchen items for a period not to exceed ten days.

1. Whenever BOR 9-2 E is executed, a note with the verbatim "Kitchen Scolding Phrase" shall be left.

PHRASEOLOGY EXAMPLE: *"You are in violation of BOR 9-2, and your small kitchen items have been temporarily removed. Your kitchen items will be returned in (period within the ten-day limit) days. Please be more considerate to your friends and family after your kitchen items have been returned."*

BOR 9-3 | Mandatory Pantry Layout

A well-kept kitchen pantry is essential to maintaining a clean and efficient kitchen. Kitchen pantries vary in size from a small cabinet to an entire separate room (in larger homes). Cabinet spaces should always be kept clean and organized. Commonly used food and kitchen items should be stored at eye level. Small kitchen appliances used less than once a month should always be stored in kitchen pantries.

A. To the extent possible, food and nonfood items should be stored on separate shelves in kitchen pantries. If insufficient pantry space makes doing so impractical, shelves may be divided with a clearly defined and obvious line (example: cups on the left and breakfast cereal on the right of a pantry shelf).

BOR 9-3. Any item with a poison-control warning label shall never be placed on a shelf that stores food.

1. For convenience, nonfood items may be stored with corresponding food items such as flour and cupcake holders.

2. Any item with a poison-control warning label shall never be placed on a shelf that stores food.

B. A supply of plastic grocery bags may be kept in a holding receptacle in kitchen pantries. Recycled grocery bags can be used as a backup for trash bags, pet cleanup and the transport of goods outside the home.

1. The total maximum number of plastic grocery store bags stored in kitchen pantries is 50, or an amount that requires 1 cubic foot of pantry space, whichever is less.

2. A recommended option for the storage of grocery store bags is the cloth bag sleeve, which may be hung on the interior door of the kitchen pantry.

BOR 9-4 | Cup Orientation in Cabinets

All cups must be placed face down in kitchen cabinets. There are obvious disadvantages to placing cups in both the up and down positions in cabinets. Placing cups open end up may result in the accumulation of dust particles, which will mix with beverages when a drink is poured. Placing cups face down directly exposes the rim of the glass to cabinet shelves, which may contain contaminants. The exposure of the small surface area of the rim is favorable to the exposure of the entire surface area of the inside of the glass.

BOR 9-4. All cups must be placed face down in kitchen cabinets.

A. The following circumstances allow a face-up placement of cups in cabinets but will ultimately result in the ingestion of airborne dust particles:

1. Drinking receptacles have an uneven glass rim resulting in a lopsided upside-down placement.

2. Cabinet shelves have an unusual design resulting in properly placed cups utilizing an inordinate amount of cabinet space.

3. Decorative cups are displayed and not intended for use.

BOR 9-5 | Authorized Drinking Receptacles

Beverages may only be served and consumed in their authorized corresponding drinking receptacle. Individual cups may be appropriate for certain types of beverages and inappropriate for others. The Authorized Drinking Receptacle List details individual beverages with their corresponding acceptable cups. Good judgment should be exercised when considering cup selection for beverages not on this list.

A. Authorized Drinking Receptacle List

1. Milk or milk-based drink: glass or paper

2. Wine: glass

3. Tea, coffee: coffee cup, styrofoam, plastic, paper

4. Juice: any receptacle except wine glass unless mixed with alcohol

5. Soda, beer and water: any drinking receptacle

B. The following exceptions to the Authorized Drinking Receptacle List are authorized, however, consuming milk from any receptacle other than glass or paper is forbidden except as outlined in BOR 9-5 B3.

1. Monetary restrictions deny individuals from a complete kitchen complement.

2. An individual is drinking beverages away from home. However, all efforts shall be exhausted to determine appropriate cup availability before consuming beverages from an unauthorized receptacle.

3. Drinking milk in a glass or paper receptacle is specifically contrary to the religious beliefs of an individual.

BOR 9-6 | The Trash Can

Trash cans, also referred to as trash bins, waste bins and trash receptacles, shall be used to contain trash within the home. One trash receptacle should be designated as primary and placed in the kitchen of every home. Secondary trash receptacles are required in every bathroom and are optional for all other rooms. All trash bins must be emptied weekly, or whenever trash levels meet or exceed the rim of the receptacle, whichever occurs first. A single individual shall be assigned the primary responsibility of trash removal within the home.

A. Kitchen trash cans may only be composed of either metal or plastic.

B. Participation in a community recycling program is mandatory when curbside pickup services are provided free of charge.

C. Tossing items of trash "basketball style" into trash receptacles is prohibited. This practice creates a mess and usually demonstrates inferior athleticism.

BOR 9-7 | The Refrigerator

Kitchen refrigerators may be adorned with small items such as photographs, children's artwork and "to-do" lists in any combination with a maximum total limit of seven items. These items should be rotated on a regular basis. Items may be displayed on the front or either side of a refrigerator. Exceeding the maximum limit of seven items significantly increases kitchen clutter.

A. Whenever kitchen refrigerators are decorated with one or more items, one of the maximum seven items shall be a household grocery list (see BOR 3-7).

B. Temporary refrigerator blindness, caused by obsessively opening and closing the door, can be treated by elevating the feet and placing a damp cloth over the eyes.

C. The little man who turns the light on and off inside refrigerators should never be disturbed. He works diligently and thanklessly for little pay.

BOR 9-8 | Stovetops and Ovens

The kitchen stove is an enclosed area to heat food. In 1742, Benjamin Franklin invented the modern kitchen stove. Stoves induct heat created by electricity, gas or fire. Ovens are used in the preparation of food by broiling, baking or roasting food. Most conventional ovens operate by circulating air at a prescribed temperature over food.

A. Kitchen stoves shall be deep cleaned at least annually, but spot cleaning should be conducted whenever food is observed on stovetops.

B. The only items authorized for storage on kitchen stovetops are salt and pepper shakers (see BOR 5-9 C) and spoon rests.

C. Pot handles shall always be turned away from the front of the stove.

D. Cloth pot holders decoratively displayed in kitchens shall either match the selected kitchen's overall decorative theme (see BOR 9-10) or be neutral in theme.

BOR 9-9 | The Microwave

Invented by accident by Percy Spencer in 1945, the microwave oven has become an invaluable appliance in the home. The American inventor was working on an unrelated experiment when he noticed that a candy bar in his pocket began to melt while he was experimenting with microwave radio signals.

Microwave ovens operate by dielectrically heating water and other polarized molecules using radiation. Microwave ovens heat food quickly and efficiently but cannot bake or brown foods as effectively as other appliances. Appropriately, the first food to be intentionally cooked in a microwave was popcorn.

A. As with all appliances that come in contact with food, microwave ovens should be cleaned regularly. The interior of microwave ovens shall be treated with a disinfectant spray or cleaned at least monthly.

B. Microwave ovens may only be operated to cook or reheat food specifically prepared for microwave ovens.

C. The individual using the microwave oven has the specific responsibility of clearing the numbers on the digital display after use.

D. The sound on microwave oven digital keypads shall always be enabled.

BOR 9-10 | Mandatory Kitchen Theme

All kitchens should be assigned an object, concept or decorative theme to represent the household. The food preparation specialist (see BOR 9-11 A) is responsible for the assignment of the kitchen decorative theme. For example, angels may be assigned as the kitchen theme. In this case, a modest number of angels may be displayed throughout the kitchen. Themed decorative kitchen items may include salt and pepper shakers (see BOR 5-9), kitchen magnets (see BOR 9-7) and decorative figurines.

A. At least two but no more than twenty items representing the selected theme shall be displayed in the kitchen.

B. It is encouraged, although not required, that additional items representing the selected theme be placed in other locations within the home.

C. Whenever the general food preparation specialist responsibilities (see BOR 9-11 A) transfer from one individual to another, the theme-selection rights immediately transfer to the new individual.

| BOR 9-11 | **The Food Preparation Specialist**

Cooking is an art usually passed down from parents and grandparents. Preparing food at home is significantly less expensive than dining out and helps ensure that healthful foods are consumed. One specific area of the kitchen should be reserved for

BOR 9-11. A rarely enforced law states that jewelry discovered in a prepared meal becomes the property of the eater.

the preparation of food. A well-organized kitchen eliminates much of the stress involved in preparing a meal.

A. The individual primarily responsible for food preparation in the home is designated as the food preparation specialist.

B. Hands must be washed before preparing food.

C. Uncooked meat may never be exposed to other foods.

D. For individuals who have a blood alcohol content beyond the legal driving limit in the state in which he or she currently resides (see BOR 11-9 A), preparing food for others is prohibited.

E. Wearing loose jewelry is prohibited during the preparation of food.

　　1. A rarely enforced law states that jewelry discovered in a prepared meal becomes the property of the eater.

BOR 9-12 | The Importance of the Family Dinner

Families today are extremely busy. Most household parents are working parents, and little time is set aside to prepare a formal meal. However, time should be allotted in the family schedule to consume at least one meal together daily. Research indicates that sitting down to dinner improves communication and helps ensure all family members routinely consume healthful foods. Utilizing the dinner table is the perfect opportunity to connect with family members, learn more about each other and discuss the events of the day.

A. A preset dinnertime shall be established and honored by all members of the home.

B. Serving individual food items disliked by one or more family members is authorized only once weekly.

C. A conversation starter such as "best and worst part of the day" is encouraged when dining with children.

BOR 9-13 | Dishwashing Principles

If food is consumed at home at least once daily, dishwashing shall occur at least once daily. The food preparation specialist (see BOR 9-11 A) has the primary responsibility of determining the time, method and persons to participate in the washing of dishes. An effort should be made by the food preparation specialist to rotate the individuals selected to wash dishes.

A. Under normal circumstances, the food preparation specialist is generally exempt from the washing of dishes.

B. Regardless of the dishwashing method, warm or hot water should always be used to wash dishes.

C. Dishwashers must be loaded carefully. Loose items such as small measuring cups should be placed in the dishwasher silverware rack. To assist in the longevity of the appliance, dishwashers should be operated at least monthly.

D. Fragile items, such as wine glasses, should never be placed in dishwashers.

BOR 9-14 | Minimum Fire Extinguisher Requirement

The fire extinguisher has changed radically since it was first introduced in England in the early seventeenth century. George Herman Manby produced the first modern fire extinguisher in 1818. This early fire-prevention device contained three gallons of ash propelled by compressed air. Most household fire extinguishers are red, with instructions clearly written on the unit. The possession of a fire extinguisher is paramount in ensuring home safety. Every member of the home should possess a general knowledge of the classes of fires and fire extinguishers. Although additional fire classifications exist, most household fire extinguishers are intended for class A, B or C fires. Class A fires involve organic materials such as paper or wood. Class B fires involve flammable liquids such as gasoline or grease. Class C fires involve flammable gasses.

A. At least one fire extinguisher shall be kept in every home. It is recommended that a fire extinguisher is maintained in all household kitchens, garages and outdoor workshops. At a minimum, one fire extinguisher shall be placed in every kitchen.

B. Every member of a household shall be verbally questioned at least annually about the location of all household fire extinguishers.

C. Home fire extinguishers must be checked quarterly to ensure a proper charge.

D. Playing fire extinguisher tag is prohibited within the home and all other locations under a roof.

DRESS

BOR 10-1 | **Age-Restricted Clothing**

Clothing items identified as "teen wear" in popular magazines and media shall not be worn by any individual over the age of twenty-three. This restriction applies both in public and private. The term *teen wear* is rather generic, and good judgment should be exercised when selecting attire.

A. The most commonly identified teen wear items are currently:

1. Baggy pants, three or more sizes too large, giving the wearer the appearance of a clown or court jester

2. "Girly" socks worn by males that extend no higher than the top of the shoe

3. Any outfit that clearly reveals underwear

4. Low-rise pants that allow the belly to hang happy and free

5. Any clothing item purchased at a mall location in which music is played at a level of 90 decibels or higher

---

BOR 10-2 | Personal Clothing Quota

All adult men and women shall establish a personal clothing quota of individual items within their wardrobe. A specific limit of clothing items—such as shirts, socks and shoes—must be established and maintained. Personal clothing quotas are not restrictive. However, good judgment should be exercised. An example of a clothing quota for a 28-year-old male would be thirty shirts, twelve pairs of pants, nine pairs of shoes and three suits. After an article of clothing is purchased, and the clothing quota for similar items has been exceeded, a similar item from an individual's clothing inventory shall be removed.

A. The disposal of the replaced clothing item shall be accomplished within seven days of the purchase of the new clothing item.

B. Donating excessive items to charity is the preferred method of disposal.

BOR 10-3 | Carrying a Wallet Correctly

The primary purpose of a wallet is to hold currency and identification. However, a wallet also serves as a fashion accessory and care should be taken to select a wallet that is both functional and stylish. Features to consider when selecting a wallet should include bifold vs. trifold, hidden compartments, storage capacity and photograph sheets.

A. The placement of bills in wallets and purses shall be face up and in ascending order from left to right. As the wallet opens, ones shall be placed first, fives next and so on. Well-organized currency assists in expediting transactions in checkout lines (see BOR 3-14) and minimizes delays. The process of checking out is reduced by an average of 48 seconds for individuals with a well-organized wallet. Over a lifetime of shopping visits, this results in the elimination of sixteen total days needlessly spent waiting in line.

  1. Wallets given as gifts shall contain at least $5 in locally accepted currency.

B. A man's wallet shall be placed in the front right pocket, and keys shall be placed in the front left pocket. The practice of carrying the wallet in a rear pocket interferes with comfort while sitting and increases the odds of becoming a victim of theft.

  1. Professional men may elect to place wallets in an interior pocket of suits and sport jackets.

BOR 10-3. A man's wallet shall be placed in the front right pocket, and keys shall be placed in the front left pocket.

2. Money clips and folded bills do not constitute wallets and may be placed in any pocket.

BOR 10-4 | Maximum Allowable Number of Shoes

Shoes are one the most important items in an individual's wardrobe. Men and women are regularly judged by their outward appearance, and shoes can make or break the look of an outfit. Shoes worn in public should be both comfortable and stylish. Shoe size should be professionally determined biannually for children and at least once in adulthood.

A. In an effort to reduce household clutter, the personal clothing quota for shoes is thirty-five pairs per individual (see BOR 10-2). Although this may sound excessive, violations of overage routinely occur, specifically with individuals who have an obsessive personality.

B. Healthy, nonhandicapped adults wearing Velcro-fastened shoes shall not be taken seriously.

C. Wearing sandals may expose the toes. In this instance, toe-nail polish, when worn, shall match fingernail polish in color, style and texture.

D. Flip-flops may only be worn outside the home at beaches, pools and amusement parks.

E. Socks and shoes should be coordinated appropriately when worn in public. Athletic shoes should be worn with tube socks, and dress shoes should be worn with dress socks. Violators of this requirement are generally middle-aged married men. The potential consequences of violating BOR 10-4 E may include, but are not limited to:

1. Sneers, laughter and other unwelcome gestures from teenagers

2. Clothing discrimination

3. A potentially embarrassing social situation in which a violator is incorrectly identified as a vagabond or drifter

F. Violators shall be tactfully notified.

PHRASEOLOGY EXAMPLE: *"Hey Harry, have you looked at your feet today?"*

BOR 10-5 | Wearing Socks With Sandals

Socks shall never be worn with sandals. Sandals are generally worn to allow air to circulate over the feet, which produces a cooling effect. Wearing socks significantly negates this process. Further, Americans are constantly videotaped, and with the popularity of the Internet, many sock-and-sandal wearers are unfortunately viewed worldwide. These individuals often symbolize American society, one of the causes of the decline of American popularity in recent years.

BOR 10-6 | Sock Guidelines

Socks absorb perspiration and keep feet moisturized. Wearing socks at night helps to prevent dry, flaky skin. Everyday socks

BOR 10-6. "Girly" socks which extend no higher than the top of the shoe (see BOR 10-1) shall not be worn by men over age twenty-three.

consist of cotton, wool or nylon, and premium softer socks consist of silk, linen or cashmere. Sock sizes typically correspond with shoe sizes. In general, the style and color of socks should match the style and color of pants and blouses.

A. "Girly" socks which extend no higher than the top of the shoe (see BOR 10-1) shall not be worn by men over age twenty-three.

B. Socks shall not be worn outside the home without shoes. Socks shall be removed before exiting the home, or shoes shall be worn over socks prior to any individual exiting a residence.

C. Temporary exceptions to style regulations BOR 10-5 and BOR 10-6 are permitted for household errands with a duration of sixty seconds or less, provided the individual does not exit the physical property they own or rent.

BOR 10-7 | Authorized Shirts

The shirt is an item of clothing worn on the upper body. Shirts are designed from natural and man-made materials. Originally worn exclusively by men, shirts have become a commonplace accessory for both sexes. Shirts should always be clean and changed after exercise or extensive physical activity.

A. Personalized T-shirts are prohibited for any individual that does not fully understand its intending meaning.

B. Souvenir shirts embossed with a specific location are only authorized for individuals who have visited the location at least once.

C. Overtly revealing or low-cut shirts should not be worn in public.

1. This practice reduces the instances of discrimination, blank stares and avoidable traffic accidents.

BOR 10-8 | Wearing Pajamas

Individuals should be dressed in "day clothing" within two hours after waking. Human dignity mandates the daily change of clothing. Pajamas may be worn in the home from shortly before bedtime until two hours after an individual awakens. Pajama wear is not permitted outside the home except for the swift retrieval of mail or the morning newspaper, or other brief activities within the yard lasting 60 seconds or less.

A. Clothing worn on the previous day constitutes pajama wear after worn to bed.

B. Individuals who sleep nude or who wear minimal pajamas shall be dressed immediately after waking.

C. A single "day-clothing free" day is authorized once per week for individuals not exiting the home. "Day-clothing free" days are permitted any day of the week that the primary job is not conducted.

D. Along with severe alcoholism and social withdrawal, wearing pajamas away from the home is a nonverbal admission that an individual has completely given up on life. Those individuals observed publicly wearing pajamas must be treated with compassion, dignity and respect.

BOR 10-9 | Jewelry Restrictions

Jewelry is an important part of an outfit that can significantly increase style. Any jewelry should complement an individual's wardrobe and personal appearance. Both age and face shape should be considered in the purchase of jewelry. Jewelry should always be appropriate for the occasion.

A. At least one holding receptacle shall be maintained to store, display and organize jewelry. Holding receptacles include jewelry boxes, ring trees and decorative candelabras.

B. Jewelry received as a gift must be worn at least once in the presence of the individual who purchased the item.

C. Loose-fitting jewelry may not be worn during the preparation of food (see BOR 9-11 E).

D. The purchase or possession of a single piece of jewelry exceeding the value of the primary family vehicle is prohibited.

E. A total number of three rings may be worn by an individual outside the home. All rings, including wedding bands and engagement rings, count toward the maximum limit of three. Excessively large or decorative rings shall be limited to one per hand.

BOR 10-10 | Hair Regulations

Hair should always be kept neat and orderly. As referenced in BOR 8-1 A2, ensuring hair is stylish and well groomed is a high priority in life. Hair should be shampooed daily, preferably by showering in the morning (see BOR 8-11). Shampoo should be quickly rinsed from the hair to prevent drying. Excessive body hair should be trimmed and maintained by all adults under fifty.

A. A full-service salon session consisting of shampoo, massage and facial shall be experienced at least once in a lifetime by all adult men and women.

BOR 10-10. Excessive hair twirling reflects, often inaccurately, inferior intelligence and is discouraged.

B. Excessive hair twirling reflects, often inaccurately, inferior intelligence and is discouraged.

   1. The nervous habit of tasting one's hair is prohibited in the presence of others.

C. Overtly extravagant haircuts or hair styles may not be given to a child without verbal consent.

D. Hair may be colored professionally or at home in any of the following six shades:

   1. Black

   2. Brown

   3. Auburn

   4. Red

5. Blonde

6. Blue

Hat Wear and Alignment

All hats keep wearers warm in the winter and cool in the summer. Fifty years ago, hats were a commonplace fashion accessory. The popularity of hats has waned; however, they are still favored by sports fans and older men seeking to camouflage a receding hairline. Hats not only protect from the elements of nature but provide an individual with a sense of dignity.

A. All hats shall be removed at any location, if and when the national anthem is played.

BOR 10-11. Sporting caps shall always be aligned either straight forward or straight reverse when worn.

B. Men's hats shall be removed at church, school, theaters and all restaurants.

C. Men's hats shall be tipped in return for gratitude received for service or assistance.

D. Sporting caps shall always be aligned either straight forward or straight reverse when worn.

BOR 10-12 | Primary Fragrance Selection

Many American men and women wear fragrance. Fragrances have evolved little since the time of the ancient Egyptians. The scent of colognes and perfumes is described as a musical metaphor with three sets of notes that combine to form the harmonious scent accord. The top notes are observed immediately after a fragrance is applied. These scents evaporate relatively quickly. The middle notes, or heart notes, are revealed after much of the water and alcohol evaporates. The heart notes generally define a specific scent. The base notes are perceived about thirty minutes after application as the cologne is absorbed into the skin. Base notes and middle notes comprise the body of a scent. A specific fragrance selection shall be determined only after analyzing the top notes, middle notes and base notes of a cologne or perfume.

A. A single cologne or perfume shall be chosen as the primary fragrance by all adults. The selected primary fragrance shall be worn with a greater consistency than any other individual fragrance.

B. Periodic changes to an individual's primary fragrance are permitted provided close friends and family members are promptly notified.

C. Fragrances shall never be worn to such a degree that a noticeable scent may be discerned from a distance of 6 feet away or greater.

BOR 10-13 | Corrective Lenses

Regular eye exams are critical in maintaining proper eye health. In addition to writing prescriptions, optometrists check for a long list of eye problems and diseases during a routine eye examination. Detecting problems early is one of the keys to ensuring lifelong eye health. Eyeglasses have significantly evolved in recent years. Lightweight, scratch-resistant eyewear is now affordable in nearly every household budget.

A. Both children and adults shall have a professional eye exam at least annually.

B. Expensive prescription sunglasses are a luxury saved for responsible adults. Designer eyewear is authorized only for individuals who can be reasonably self assured that eyeglasses will not be broken or misplaced within six months of purchase.

C. Individuals who routinely wear eyeglasses shall be familiar with the procedure of using only sunlight and eyeglasses to create fire. This knowledge proves invaluable if one is selected to appear on a reality-based survival TV show.

BOR 10-14 | Watch Placement

Whenever a watch is worn in public, it shall be worn on the wrist opposite the preferred writing hand, facing outward. Wearing a watch with the timepiece facing inward forces the wearer to turn the wrist inward to view the time. Statistically, watch wearers

BOR 10-14. Whenever a watch is worn in public, it shall be worn on the wrist opposite the preferred writing hand, facing outward.

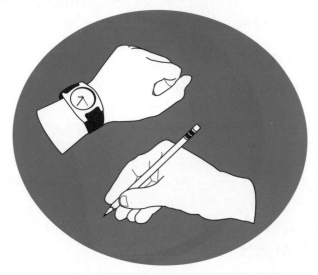

glance at their watch 18.266 times daily. The annual energy wasted in needless wrist-turning, multiplied by 18.266, multiplied by the number of watch wearers in North America would power the city of Waterloo, Illinois, for nine weeks.

MULTIMEDIA

| **BOR 11-1** | **Enhancing the Movie Theater Experience** |

When attending a movie theater, all adult members of a group should make their movie selection prior to arrival. When planning an evening consisting of dinner and a movie, the movie should be viewed before dinner. Whenever a movie is viewed after dining, sufficient hunger does not exist to thoroughly enjoy theater food items such as nachos and popcorn. Further, the inevitable burping (see BOR 6-5), farting (see BOR 6-4) and tooth-picking (see BOR 5-14) noises cause unnecessary distractions in the theater.

A. Optimal movie viewing is experienced in the center of the last row of the theater. This position allows features to be viewed at a slight downward angle providing maximum comfort. The center rear seats are positioned to allow the greatest audio range from advanced audio sound systems. Additionally, ambient noise from other movie patrons is significantly reduced and often eliminated. Theater seat selection shall be as close as possible to this last row position.

BOR 11-1. A movie should be viewed before dinner to ensure sufficient hunger for theater food items. Unnecessary distractions in the theater are also prohibited.

B. All feature-length motion pictures should be viewed in sequence in movie theaters. Watching movies in sequence increases understanding and reduces the probability of moviegoers causing distractions by asking plot questions during a film. For example, it is strictly forbidden to view *Why I Like Yarn PART III* before Parts I and II are viewed.

C. Applause is mandatory after the viewing of a film that an individual personally considers exceptional.

D. Screaming the word *bingo* is expressly forbidden in the viewing area of a movie theater after the lights have dimmed.

BOR 11-2 | Complaints About Movie Commercials

The practice of airing commercials before a feature presentation has become commonplace. This will not be tolerated. Immediately after the completion of a film, each ticket holder shall personally complain to management whenever commercials were viewed prior to the airing of the movie. Along with voting, jury duty and community service, this is a primary civic duty of every American. With widespread adherence of this regulation, the practice of airing theater commercials will ultimately be terminated.

A. An alternate delivery of complaints may be accomplished by telephone, mail, e-mail or in person. This shall be accomplished by each ticket holder within 24 hours of the completion of a feature presentation.

   PHRASEOLOGY EXAMPLES:

   1. *"I didn't just pay $9.50 to watch ads for soap."*

   2. *"Don't you make enough money from the $5 sodas?"*

   3. *"My uncle Gary is a lot bigger than you. He hates paying $5 for a soda, and really bad things happen when he is forced to watch ads for soap."*

B. A BOR D-1 Discrepancy Form (see BOR Appendix A) shall be included with all written complaints.

BOR 11-3 | Maximum Allowable Television Viewing Time

It is recommended that individuals make cable or satellite television available in the home to provide a wide variety of options for viewers. To the maximum extent possible, television commercials should not be viewed. Advertisements corrode the mind and should be avoided. Electronic recording equipment, such as DVR, may be utilized to meet this requirement.

A. Television may be watched up to a maximum of 4 hours daily. If any amount of television is viewed throughout the day, some portion must consist of nonfictional programs such as news, documentaries or discussion.

B. Television commercial viewing is allowable during major sporting events such as the Super Bowl. Multimillion dollar commercials are often more entertaining than the sporting event itself.

C. The time spent watching television counts toward the maximum allowable time playing video games (see BOR 11-14).

D. Two or more television programs should always be queued for viewing. This allows the option of switching between programs during commercial breaks. Watching only one television program at a time indicates poor television planning and is strongly discouraged.

BOR 11-4 | Preferred News Media

Local newspapers shall be the preferred media to obtain local news and current events. Newspapers typically offer a wider variety and more detailed information than other sources, such as Internet and radio. At least one newspaper shall be purchased weekly. Home delivery is preferable to purchasing issues away from home unless a specific operational advantage exists when purchasing a paper at a newsstand or elsewhere.

BOR 11-4. The preferred method of expired newspaper disposal is recycling, where available.

A. Newspapers are considered expired two weeks after printed.

B. Expired newspapers may not be retained in the home unless a specific article, photograph or announcement pertains to an individual who has a personal relationship with the reader.

C. The preferred method of expired newspaper disposal is recycling, where available (see BOR 9-6 B).

BOR 11-5 | Maximum Allowable Number of DVDs

The total number of prerecorded DVDs retained in the home shall be minimized to the extent possible. Excessive DVD collections contribute to clutter and disorganization within the home. Each individual within a household is allowed up to a maximum of twenty prerecorded DVDs when a video rental store operates within 15 miles of the home.

A. Personally recorded DVDs do not apply toward the limit of twenty and may be retained without restriction.

B. Individuals residing more than 15 miles from an operational video rental store may possess an unlimited number of DVDs without restriction.

BOR 11-6 | Telephone Etiquette

At least one telephone shall be kept in every occupied bedroom in the home. When answering the phone at home, the identity of a caller shall be determined and expressed before handing the phone to the designated recipient. The precious few moments of preparation between an individual receiving the phone and initial vocal exchange prepare the phone call recipient for conversation. Simple phrases such as, "It's Tom," or "Jimmy wants to talk to you" are acceptable.

A. After an individual is advised of the identity of a caller, they have the option of receiving the call.

B. Phone call recipients shall directly refer to the caller by name, if known. Example: "Hello, Tom," or "Hello, Jimmy."

C. Call-waiting shall be used with discretion. No one appreciates losing a call-waiting face-off.

1. When answering a secondary call, the maximum transfer time is 30 seconds before switching back to the original caller. Example: "Hi, Rebecca. I am on the other line. I'll call you back in 10 minutes."

2. After returning to the original caller, the disruption shall be acknowledged. Example: "I apologize for the interruption. You were telling me about … "

D. Telephone calls may not be placed between the hours of 10 P.M. and 6 A.M. in the time zone of the recipient unless an emergency condition exits.

E. Three specific actions are prohibited when using a telephone at home.

1. Chewing gum
2. The consumption of food
3. Flushing the toilet

NOTE: Using the restroom while on the telephone is permissible. However, flushing the toilet may be accomplished only after the completion of the call.

BOR 11-7 | Terminating Phone Calls

Proper etiquette shall be exercised on all telephone calls. All rules associated with face-to-face conversation apply to phone conversation. However, it may be difficult to find a break in conversation when communicating with a verbose individual. This may create complications when attempting to terminate a phone conversation. In this case, telephone conversations may be terminated in one of two ways:

A. Abruptly and politely speaking over the other individual, using a phrase such as, "I've got to go."

B. Pressing the number 9 on the telephone keypad at gradually increasing intervals. This action hinders communication

BOR 11-7. When on a call with a verbose individual, the call may be terminated by pressing the number 9 on the telephone keypad at gradually increasing intervals.

sufficiently to allow an individual to verbalize a request to terminate the call.

BOR 11-8 | Mobile Phone Etiquette

Individuals operating mobile phones in public shall maintain situational awareness. Mobile phone users should be receptive to the conversation and body language of others while engaging in cell phone conversation. The public operation of mobile phones shall be conducted in a professional and courteous manner. The following list of mobile phone procedures is mandated whenever a mobile phone is operated in public:

A. Live conversation takes precedence over cell phone conversation.

B. An apologetic statement shall be spoken before live conversation is interrupted to engage in cell phone conversation.

PHRASEOLOGY EXAMPLE: *"Excuse me; I've got a call."*

C. Mobile phone conversation shall be abruptly terminated whenever any situation develops that may require the complete attention of a cell phone user.

D. Mobile phones may not be utilized whenever conversation may hinder driving (see BOR 2-4).

E. Subjects inappropriate for face-to-face public conversation are also inappropriate while using a mobile phone in public.

F. Making direct eye contact with another individual is prohibited while operating a hands-free phone except as prescribed in BOR 2-1.

BOR 11-9 | Alcohol and Written Electronic Messages

The transmission of written electronic messages is prohibited whenever an individual has a blood alcohol content beyond the legal driving limit in the state in which he or she currently resides. Electronic messages consist of text messages, e-mail or any other media in which written text is instantly transmitted to one or more individuals.

A. Self Sobriety Test: When electronic alcohol sensors are not available, self sobriety may be determined by reciting the Pledge of Allegiance aloud, without error, in 7 seconds or less.

B. Electronic messages may be composed while under the influence of alcohol provided transmission does not occur until complete sobriety is reached.

BOR 11-9. Self sobriety may be determined by reciting the Pledge of Allegiance aloud, without error, in 7 seconds or less.

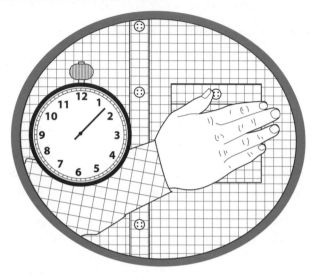

BOR 11-10 | E-Mail Etiquette

E-mail shall be considered formal communication. Every transmitted message should contain a subject, salutation and signature. All e-mail messages should be grammatically correct. The spell-check feature shall be used, when available, before each message is transmitted. When operating e-mail applications without a spell-check feature, the document shall be briefly scanned for errors before transmission.

A. Unsolicited e-mail shall not be forwarded unless the message contains information specifically pertinent to the recipient. All nonpertinent text should be removed before transmittal.

B. Unsolicited e-mails with attachments of 1MB or larger may not be transmitted to a recipient with a known dial-up Internet connection without prior permission.

C. The Blind Carbon Copy (or BCC) e-mail function shall be utilized when e-mailing multiple recipients to prevent disclosing the e-mail address of all recipients. This feature masks the identity of the other recipients of the e-mail.

   1. Blind carbon copy is optional if the identity of all e-mail recipients is intentionally disclosed.

D. A small segment of the American population known as "Forward Folk" suffer from a obsessive mental condition that causes them to compulsively forward the web address of every website they visit each day to every individual in their address list. Although only 4 percent of the web population, Forward Folk transmit nearly 45 percent of all e-mails worldwide. Every effort shall be made to politely discourage Forward Folk from their next binge mass e-mail transmission.

   PHRASEOLOGY EXAMPLE: *"Steve, I'd really like to see the video you watched last night with the bear juggling those cats, but I just don't have time for that right now. Have you thought about playing tennis? I've heard the cardiovascular benefits are incredible."*

BOR 11-11 | Social Networking Websites

Social networking websites have evolved into an interactive platform to communicate with friends and family. Networking sites allow individuals to create detailed profiles and seek out and communicate with others online. Most networking sites offer interactive applications and games accessed by multiple individuals across the country and the globe.

A. To help ensure privacy, public profiles should contain minimal personal information.

B. Only one social networking web game requiring daily interaction may be played at a time.

C. Individuals using a social website for dating purposes shall ensure the primary profile photo was taken within the previous year.

D. Interactive life simulation and farming-based web games are authorized for any individual with at least one other hobby.

BOR 11-12 | Texting Etiquette

Texting shall be considered informal communication. Messages may contain sentence fragments, symbols and abbreviations. Texting is only authorized after verbal communication has been established. For example, texting a co-worker whom an individual has never called is not authorized. There are no preset limits assigned to text messages, yet consideration shall be given to others when multiple texts are transmitted.

A. Texting is authorized only for individuals separated by a distance of 200 feet or more.

B. Regardless of federal and state law, texting while driving is forbidden. This practice is extremely dangerous and an unglamorous method of suicide.

C. Forwarding unsolicited cell phone text messages is forbidden, unless the forwarded message specifically pertains to the recipient.

D. When an individual feels harassed by another due to an inordinate number of text messages received, the "texting termination abbreviation" may be transmitted to the sender. The texting termination abbreviation consists of the first letter of each word of the texting termination phrase:

TEXTING TERMINATION ABBREVIATION:
"IHEOTIHALAYSTPPUTPACMIYWTCFTYVM"

TEXTING TERMINATION PHRASE: *"I've had enough of this. I have a life, and you should too. Please pick up the phone and call me if you wish to communicate further. Thank you very much."*

BOR 11-12. Regardless of federal and state law, texting while driving is forbidden. This practice is extremely dangerous and an unglamorous method of suicide.

BOR 11-13 | Illegally Altering Home Computer Settings

Millions of dollars are spent annually replacing computer monitors destroyed by angry computer users after home computer settings have been illegally altered. One individual shall be designated as the primary user for every personal computer in the home. Personal computer settings may be only altered by the owner or primary user. Computer owners may designate to others the authority to make changes to computer settings. Such designations may be written or verbal.

PHRASEOLOGY EXAMPLE: *"Hey Eddie, feel free to change the fonts and backgrounds when you use my computer. But I've got to warn you, if you install that roving pink unicorn theme on my desktop again, I'm going to hunt you down and remove the hair from your head."*

BOR 11-14 | Maximum Allowable Video Game Time

Video games are electronic applications that combine human interaction with a computerized device and provide visual feedback on a display. A.S. Douglas invented the first graphical video game, a simple version of tic-tac-toe, in 1952. Modern video games are designed by scores of engineers and computer programmers who often provide a realistic simulation of strange new worlds.

A. No more than 4 hours per day may be spent playing video games.

    1. The time spent playing video games counts toward the maximum allowable time watching television (see BOR 11-3).

B. The body movement conducted while playing video games, regardless of intensity, does not count as physical exercise.

BOR 11-14. The time spent playing video games counts toward the maximum allowable time watching television, and may not exceed 4 hours.

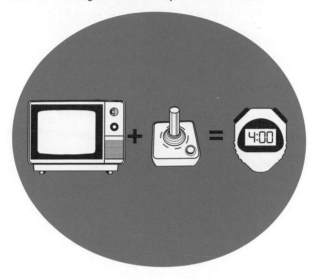

BOR 11-15 | Singing Aloud With Headphones

Headphones are used to prevent disturbing others while listening to music or media. Headphones also enhance audio and restrict noise pollution. Modern noise canceling headphones further restrict ambient sounds by transmitting an electronic "antinoise" signal. Popular varieties of headphones are ear covering headphones, headsets and earbuds.

A. Singing along with music while wearing headphones may never be louder than a normal singing voice.

B. Singing along with music while wearing headphones is only authorized when the singer is relatively knowledgeable of the song lyrics. Individuals signing song lyrics in error shall be courteously advised of lyrical mistakes.

C. Common Song Lyric Errors:

1. Creedence Clearwater Revival – "Bad Moon Rising"

   a. Correct: "There's a bad moon on the rise"
   b. Common Error: "There's a bathroom on the right"

2. Jimi Hendrix – "Purple Haze"

   a. Correct: "Excuse me while I kiss the sky"
   b. Common Error: "Excuse me while I kiss this guy"

3. The Beatles – "All My Loving"

   a. Correct: "All my loving, I will send to you"
   b. Common Error: "All my luggage, I will send to you"

12

THE WORKPLACE

BOR 12-1 | **Finding the Right Job**

Selecting a career that matches an individual's personality and style is one of the most critical decisions in life. The average worker spends one-quarter of his or her life (40 out of 168 hours a week) at work. As America grows and evolves, today's workplace environment is completely different than it was only fifty years ago.

A. Regardless of age, every individual shall be either working at their dream job or taking steps to achieve their dream job within five years after entering the workforce.

B. The decision about a specific career path should never be made solely based upon compensation. The following factors should always be considered in the determination of a career:

   1. Location and commute requirements
   2. Compensation, including salary, benefits and bonuses
   3. Job security
   4. The level of brownnosing required for career advancement

BOR 12-1. The average worker spends one-quarter of his or her life at work. The following factors should be considered in the determination of a career.

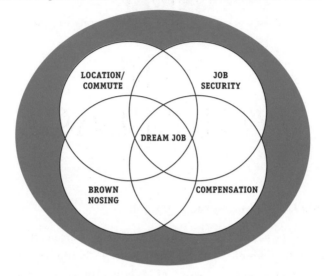

| **BOR 12-2** | **Perfecting the Language of the Résumé** |

The résumé is a formal listing of work experience and education used for seeking employment. Employers review the résumés of applicants to determine initial qualifications. Job applicants should possess both a physical and an electronic version of his or her personal résumé, as many companies require online applications.

A. Personal résumés shall be exactly one or exactly two pages in length.

B. The language of the résumé is always formal. The use of abbreviations is authorized only when their meaning would be obvious to the interviewer.

C. One tailor-fit résumé should be composed for every job application.

D. Work history should be reflected honestly, clearly and concisely. Past experience should be factually translated from plain language into the language of the résumé. For example, a recent college graduate with little or no work experience could reasonably translate, "I barely graduated and spent most of my free time as the designated driver at wild parties" into:

- Bachelor of Arts degree focusing on communication

- Effectively interacted with others

- Selflessly served as a member of a team that promoted safety and the accomplishment of objectives and goals

| BOR 12-3 | **Job Interview Tips**

Prior experience, education and interview etiquette are the three most important factors by which managers evaluate and select new employees. Managers use the interview process to ascertain the interpersonal skills of an applicant. A job candidate's character is almost always determined by the success of the interview.

A. Always be punctual for the interview. Arriving late demonstrates an individual's belief that his or her time is more important than the interviewer's time.

B. Dress slightly better for the interview than potential future co-workers.

C. Avoid discussing salary or wages unless specifically prompted by the interviewer.

D. Answer all questions honestly and concisely. Make eye contact throughout the interview process.

E. Tattoos and body piercings shall never be visible during the interview. Unfortunately, this will require certain individuals to attend job interviews wearing a bag over their head.

F. Overtly personal statements may negatively impact the interview and are discouraged.

PHRASEOLOGY EXAMPLE: *"I know your daughter, Julia, is dismissed at 3:40 from McCartney Elementary School on West 14th Street, and I would like a job please."*

BOR 12-3. Tattoos and body piercings shall never be visible during the interview.

BOR 12-4 | Effective Workplace Communication

Effective workplace communication fosters an environment of trust, efficiency and productivity. Achievements and expectations should be clearly and honestly communicated to both subordinates and supervisors. Most American workers are part of a team, and every effort shall be made to support, protect and encourage every member of the workplace team. Interactive communication helps meet this goal.

A. Electronic communication shall be accomplished regularly between supervisors and subordinates. All office communication shall be considered formal. Outgoing electronic messages should be briefly scanned for errors before transmission, and the spell-checker shall be used when available (see BOR 11-10).

B. Verbal communication shall be conducted courteously and professionally. Always listen while communicating, whether addressing the company president or a subordinate. Active and interactive communication reduces and often eliminates office conflict.

C. Written communication shall always be formal. Effective communication is the cornerstone of success. At least one employee in each organization shall be assigned the additional duty of serving as the translation specialist. The bilingual translation specialist shall be fluent in both English and Management. The intended "translated" meaning of formal written communication from management shall be relayed to all employees in a timely manner. Here's an example.

WRITTEN MANAGEMENT COMMUNICATION:
The management wishes to express our sincerest gratitude for your dedication and hard work on Project X. We know that all

employees will be up to the challenge in the demanding year ahead. Project X is anticipated to be completed six months ahead of schedule. The pride of completing such a massive project will be shared by all employees equally.

PLAIN ENGLISH TRANSLATION:
We expect all of you to work much harder on Project X. Working extended hours will be required with little or no time off until this thing is done. And don't even think about requesting a day off. A large bonus is offered for completing this project early. I plan to purchase a new Saab, and each of you will receive a T-Shirt embossed with the company logo. Thank you in advance for a job well done.

BOR 12-5 | The Supervisor Proximity Alert Phrase

An effort shall be made to alert co-workers whenever a supervisor is in close proximity. A predetermined "Supervisor Proximity Alert Phrase" shall be established to notify others that management ears may be listening. After hearing the supervisor proximity alert phrase, all small talk and gossip (see BOR 12-13) shall terminate immediately until the all-clear sign is given. For example, the coded supervisor proximity alert phrase "pork chops and applesauce" may be utilized to alert employees of an approaching supervisor.

A. Specific alert phrases should be simple and easy to remember.

B. The alert phrase shall be changed within 24 hours, if revealed to any member of management.

C. Changes to the current supervisor proximity alert phrase should be communicated to all employees as soon as practical.

BOR 12-6 | Increasing Productivity

Productive employees are almost always motivated employees. It is critical to determine your specific goals and work to meet those goals. Individuals seeking career advancement will work differently than those who are simply seeking a higher wage or salary. Generally, productive employees are retained and non-productive employees may face layoffs or termination.

A. Individuals seeking career advancement to management should spend at least a small portion of the workweek assigning labels and catchphrases to activities and procedures in the organization.

B. Regardless of the quality or quantity of work accomplished, all employees shall ensure they "appear to be working" throughout the entire workday.

   1. Creatively avoiding work is strictly prohibited whenever the effort required to avoid work is greater than the effort to accomplish work.

BOR 12-7 | Negotiating and Managing Pay

Pay should be negotiated and clearly understood before beginning work at a new job. Employee compensation programs including retirement and flexible spending accounts shall be thoroughly reviewed during the first four weeks of employment. A reasonable budget shall be established and followed within eight weeks after the first paycheck.

A. Excessive payday splurging and shopping sprees are discouraged, although not prohibited.

BOR 12-7. Excessive payday splurging and shopping sprees are discouraged although not prohibited.

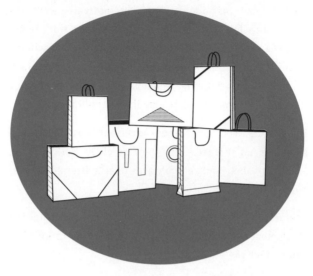

B. The investment practice entitled "Pay Yourself First" can be accomplished painlessly through payroll deduction. A predetermined amount or percentage shall be deducted from the paycheck and directly deposited into a retirement savings account or investment.

    1. The minimum required monthly contribution to a retirement account is an individual's age divided by the number 5. For example, a forty-year-old woman should contribute 8 percent or more of monthly income into a personal retirement account.

C. Payday loan services are permissible only for emergency situations and as a last resort. Many payday loans carry annual interest rates of 1000 percent or more.

1. The routine use of payday loan services is prohibited. This practice is most often conducted by individuals with a strong dislike of money. Directly discarding currency in a waste receptacle is only slightly more effective in the reduction of wealth than patronizing payday loan establishments.

BOR 12-8 | Minimizing Brownnosing

A *brownnoser* is defined as an individual who sucks up to authority for the purpose of gaining the approval of supervisors and managers. Effectively communicating with superiors is critical in career advancement, yet there is a fine line between honest communication and brownnosing. Brownnosers foster jealousy and animosity in the workplace. Managers and supervisors shall always be treated with respect; however, empty and unjustified compliments are prohibited in the workplace.

PHRASEOLOGY EXAMPLE: *"I like your plaid tie, Mr. Peterson. It really reflects your dedication and commitment to excellence in the organization."*

BOR 12-9 | The Right Way to Call in Sick

Using a sick day for an actual illness demonstrates poor leave management skills and is generally discouraged. Taking an occasional break from work can recharge and refresh an individual and assist with sanity retention. Sick days may be taken without guilt when conducted rationally and considerately.

A. Never use a sick day if your presence might be required for a unique function or task on a specific day.

B. Never frequent a restaurant, store or establishment where a co-worker may be encountered on a sick day.

C. Never lie when calling in sick. Use general and honest statements on the phone.

   PHRASEOLOGY EXAMPLE: *"I don't think I can make it in to work today. I need to take a sick day."*

D. Avoid using a gravelly old man voice when calling in sick. You sound like you are using a gravelly old man voice.

BOR 12-10 Job Transfers

In the twenty-first century, many individuals are not only forced to change jobs but also to change careers several times over a lifetime. Job transfers may be a requirement for career advancement. Often detrimental to family life, job transfers should not be considered before addressing the impact on the entire family. Individuals with children should attempt to restrict successive job transfers within a span of 3 years or fewer.

BOR 12-11 Avoiding Tardiness

Arriving late for work increases stress and negatively impacts an individual's career. Tardiness also creates a significant distraction at the beginning of the workday. For many, the snooze button on the alarm clock may serve as the biggest roadblock in career progression. Every effort shall be made to arrive at work on time. A quality alarm clock and day planner are a wise investment for everyone.

A. Never argue with supervisors after arriving late for work. Take responsibility for your tardiness and apologize honestly.

BOR 12-11. The purchase of donuts for co-workers and supervisors shall excuse any nonroutine instance of tardiness of 30 minutes or fewer.

SUGGESTED TARDINESS EXCUSES:

1. "Traffic on the interstate was terrible this morning."

2. "My three-year-old isn't well. I got here as soon as I could." (Only recommended for individuals with children.)

3. "Technically, I'm not late. I'm just REALLY early for the day shift tomorrow."

B. After it is determined that you will arrive late for work, do not rush. Additional complications such as speeding tickets or automobile accidents will only worsen the situation.

C. The purchase of donuts for co-workers and supervisors shall excuse any nonroutine instance of tardiness of 30 minutes or fewer.

Part-Time Employment

Part-time jobs are often desired for a variety of reasons. Teenagers work part-time as they enter the workforce. Adults may desire to supplement income, and older adults may desire to work after retirement. Entry-level positions also allow younger workers to earn an income while pursuing an education or training for a career. Part-time workers may elect to work for others or work from home. Part-time jobs are typically easier to find and more rewarding than full-time jobs.

A. Unless an immediate financial need exists, part-time jobs should be selected with a specific interest to an individual.

B. Parents shall ensure all children have at least one part-time job before age eighteen.

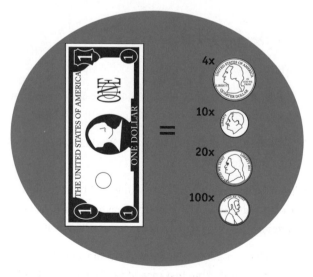

BOR 12-12. Parents should make every effort to ensure children learn the value of a dollar before leaving the home.

C. Parents should make every effort to ensure children learn the value of a dollar before leaving the home.

NOTE: Although subject to change, at the time of publication of this book, the value of a dollar is currently one hundred cents.

BOR 12-13 | Preventing Workplace Gossip

Gossip is defined as idle talk about the personal affairs of others. Careless small talk, often untrue, hinders productivity and creates a hostile work environment for all employees. Often started innocently, office gossip can transform the knowledge of a co-worker's speeding ticket into his arrest and conviction of a DWI. Gossip is not always negative. When conducted privately and professionally, gossip can be a productive way to interact with others and remain informed (especially when it comes to unadvertised information about the company).

A. If a co-worker begins a sentence with the phrase, "I really shouldn't be telling you this, but...," take a mental note. This individual shall be placed on the "do not share personal information with" list.

B. Negative personal gossip may not be shared with others. Negative personal gossip consists of any information specific to an employee which is:

1. Cruel
2. Possibly untrue
3. Unfairly or racially motivated

C. To reduce workplace gossip and protect privacy, workplace documents containing personal information shall be stored in a locked location away from the primary work location.

D. Documents containing sensitive information should be clearly marked as appropriate.

EXAMPLES:

1. Confidential
2. Secret
3. Not to be shared with Deloris in Accounts Receivable

BOR 12-14 | Office Party Conduct

Office parties shall always be considered a work function. Office parties provide invaluable networking opportunities generally not available during routine office functions. Alcohol consumption shall be limited, and individuals should always be well behaved during office parties. Plan to arrive on time or early, and leave before the party ends.

A. Attendance to optional office parties is always mandatory.

B. A total maximum limit of one alcoholic drink may be consumed every 2 hours at office parties.

C. Conversation about the workplace is prohibited unless specifically initiated by a superior.

D. The consumption of food should be conducted conservatively and slowly.

1. The request for a doggy bag is prohibited.

E. The unsolicited use of cameras or video recording devices is prohibited at office parties unless:

1. A co-worker is physically wearing a lamp shade as a hat.

2. Alcohol-induced dancing skills are demonstrated by a co-worker.

3. A co-worker is physically unable to pronounce his or her name due specifically to the effects of alcohol.

NOTE: Pictures and videos may be shared with others. However, physical photographs and electronic files shall not be given to other individuals. The electronic posting of pictures and videos on the Internet is prohibited.

BOR 12-15 | Sleeping at Work

Although discouraged by many employers, the workplace power nap significantly reduces stress and increases the ability to concentrate. Additionally, power naps increase productivity in the second half of the workday. To increase effectiveness, power naps should be taken between the fourth and fifth hour of the workday. Power naps should be taken away from the primary work location and at times of reduced workplace activity. Co-workers shall be conscientious of one another whenever power napping is in progress (see BOR 12-5).

BOR 12-16 | Reserving Workplace Lunches

Most working adults consume an inadequate breakfast or simply skip breakfast entirely. A nutritional lunch is often the most important meal of the day. A well-balanced lunch improves health and significantly increases workplace productivity. Lunches should be consumed free of distractions and away from the primary workplace when practical. Although often restricted by individual job requirements, at least 30 minutes a day should be reserved for lunch each workday.

BOR 12-16. Lunch items stored in common areas of the workplace shall be considered shared unless clearly annotated with a name or initials.

A. In an effort to reduce stress, discussions with co-workers concerning the workplace are prohibited during lunch breaks.

B. Lunch items stored in a locker or on a personal desk shall always be considered reserved.

C. Lunch items stored in a workplace refrigerator or on a lunch-room table or in other common areas shall be considered shared unless clearly annotated with a name or initials.

D. Lunch items stored without a name or initials in any work-place commons area may be consumed by Melvin at any time throughout the workday.

   1. All workplaces have at least one "Melvin." Melvin is the fictitious name assigned to the workplace food scrounger. Melvins can be easily identified as slightly overweight,

politically vocal and with a very distinct, although not necessarily unpleasant, body odor.

BOR 12-17 | Conducting Personal Business at Work

Conducting personal business during the workday distracts from the duties of the job. Conducting personal business at work costs employers millions of dollars annually. Additionally, avoiding work usually means that a fellow worker will have to pick up the slack. Personal business should be kept to a minimum in the workplace.

A. Conducting personal business at work shall always be done privately and discretely. The supervisor proximity alert phrase shall be used as necessary to protect fellow employees (see BOR 12-5).

BOR 12-17. Conducting personal business at work is always discouraged in the primary workplace, unless it concerns the sale and promotion of Girl Scout cookies.

B. Conducting personal business at work is always discouraged in the primary workplace, unless it concerns the sale and promotion of Girl Scout cookies.

C. Personal grooming should never be conducted at work. An injury sustained by stray toenails from an individual clipping at work is not considered a workplace injury.

BOR 12-18 | Quitting a Job

In the twenty-first-century workplace, it is often necessary to transition from one career to another over a lifetime of employment. It is critical that employees of every age take steps toward attaining their dream job (see BOR 12-1). Many individuals are forced to change jobs ten times or more before reaching that goal. Quitting a job is simply a part of the career progression required for an individual to find his or her specific dream job. Quitting a job should always be done tastefully and professionally.

A. Begin looking for different employment when the stress of your current job starts to affect your personal life.

B. Never quit a job before another position has been definitively secured.

C. Resigning from any job shall always be done in writing.

D. Retain a good relationship with your previous employer. You never know when you might need to go back through an open door.

E. Resigning from any job to work from home is discouraged until a specific home-based business is already profitable.

   NOTE: Most self-employed individuals do not like their boss.

13

TRAVEL

BOR 13-1 | Airports

The airport can be a stressful place. Most airports were designed to facilitate the parking of aircraft in rows rather than to accommodate airline passengers. The layout of larger airports is often complex and confusing. Increased security changes have added to the complexity of airline travel. Be sure to review airline policy concerning food, the layout of the airport and travel restrictions at least 24 hours in advance to alleviate travel-day stress.

A. Due to the frequent unavailability of wi-fi services at airports, ensure all online business is completed prior to traveling.

B. Departure gate information should be determined prior to arrival.

C. Boarding passes shall be printed online prior to arrival at the airport, when traveling with children.

D. All travelers shall actively listen to messages and announcements broadcast in airport terminals. All U.S. commercial airports are assigned a three-letter identifier. For example, the identifier for Santé Fe, New Mexico, is "SAF." All travelers shall be familiar with the identifier for both the departure and destination airports.

E. Carry-on baggage should contain at least one snack and one toy per child, when traveling with children.

F. Typically the worst part of the airport experience is "other travelers." Whenever flying, enjoy the ride and make every effort not to be an "other traveler."

BOR 13-2 | Airplanes

Traveling by commercial airline is the most expeditious method for traveling long distances. Commercial aircraft vary widely from small propeller-driven aircraft to larger jet-driven aircraft. Larger jets fly much faster and provide a significantly smoother ride. The cost of flying has increased in recent years due to higher fuel costs. Purchasing airline tickets three weeks or more in advance will provide a significant discount over purchasing tickets at the gate.

A. The removal of shoes on an aircraft is prohibited if any adjacent seat is occupied.

B. Routine conversation with neighboring passengers is only authorized after neighboring passengers initiate eye contact.

C. Due to heightened security in a confined space, the minimum requirements to board a commercial airline are now:

1. The possession of a boarding pass
2. The possession of a valid state or government issued ID
3. Passengers must have showered (see BOR 8-11) within 24 hours of the aircraft's scheduled departure time

BOR 13-2. Passengers must have showered (see BOR 8-11) within 24 hours of the aircraft's scheduled departure time.

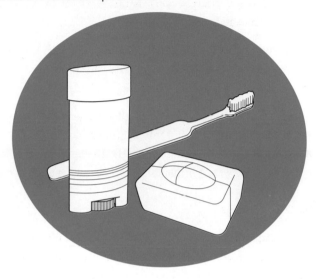

BOR 13-3 | Rental Cars

Rental cars are an inexpensive transportation option when traveling away from home. Most rental companies offer substantial savings when vehicles are booked more than one week in advance. Booking early also increases the chances of securing a specific or requested vehicle. Most rental companies require a credit card and rent vehicles to individuals who are 25 and older.

A. Inspect the vehicle thoroughly before exiting the lot. You might be responsible for preexisting vehicle damages.

B. Always ensure all drivers are included on the contract. Allowing unnamed drivers to operate a rental car may void the contract.

C. Additional insurance is usually unnecessary. Personal car insurance almost always covers rentals. Verify auto coverage before renting a car.

D. Before driving off the lot, familiarize yourself with the basic operations of the vehicle. At minimum, check the position of the headlights, wipers and emergency brake.

E. Always ask the attendant about a free upgrade to a Porsche. Rental car staff never tire of this lighthearted request. Additionally, most attendants enjoy the challenge of working with customers who are simultaneously operating a cell phone.

BOR 13-4 | Hotels

Selecting the right hotel is one of the most important decisions when traveling. Factors such as location, cost and amenities should be considered before choosing a hotel. If possible, hotel selection should be accomplished before beginning a trip. Travel websites assist individuals to reach this goal. Read all of the hotel reviews before selecting a specific hotel.

A. Always bring your own shampoo while traveling. This practice helps reduce the instances of "hotel hair."

B. Guests should be honest and fair about paying for damages incurred while staying in a hotel. Excuses such as, "The television was already hanging out the window by the cord when I checked in!" are generally not accepted.

C. Whenever possible, hotels shall be selected with a quality score of 125 points or more. The hotel quality score is determined by the Hotel Quality Chart.

1. Hotel Quality Chart

ALL HOTELS BEGIN WITH A BASE SCORE OF 100 POINTS	
+5	for a well-maintained indoor pool
+10	for an on-site restaurant or room services provided
+10	if ground transportation is provided free of charge
+20	if premium coffee is provided free of charge
+25	for a professional and courteous staff
-1	for each minute an individual is required to wait at check-in
-1	for each missing hub cap in the parking lot
-10	for each missing or inoperative appliance in the room
-15	if coffee is not provided
-20	for each improperly placed roll of toilet paper in the room or lobby (see BOR 8-1 C)

D. The minimum tip for the bellhop is one dollar per piece of luggage plus fifty cents for each instance that a bellhop personally refers to you as "Sir" or "Ma'am," provided your gender is correctly guessed.

E. It is illegal to purchase a hotel until all properties of a given color are owned and four green houses are purchased.

BOR 13-5 | **Cruises**

A cruise travel vacation is an excellent option for individuals seeking rest and relaxation. Cruises offer activities for every

BOR 13-4. It is illegal to purchase a hotel until all properties of a given color are owned and four green houses are purchased.

age from the elderly to young children. Life looks a little different from the deck of a luxury liner. Spending a week or two waking up in a different location each day is an adventure everyone should experience at least once. A cruise vacation is the perfect way to get away from life for a little while.

A. To avoid delays and complications, passports should be obtained before booking a cruise.

B. Although humorous, references to the Titanic shall not be made while on board.

C. Animals are not permitted on cruise ships.

   1. The only two exceptions to this rule are certified service dogs and animals smuggled in with the luggage.

D. Bringing alcohol on board a cruise is prohibited.

   1. A possible solution to this problem involves an empty
      mouthwash bottle and a little creativity.

BOR 13-6 | Taxicabs

Taxicabs are vehicles for hire for single passengers or small
groups. Typically operating in urban areas, taxicabs are an efficient and inexpensive mode of transportation. Most taxicabs
display a "vacant" sign when available for hire. Passengers shall
fully understand the fee structure before hailing a taxicab, and
have enough currency to pay for the ride.

A. Care should be taken to select a taxicab with a safe driver.
   This information can be accurately determined by observ-
   ing the number of hand-prints and face prints on the
   Plexiglas divider.

B. Conversation initiated by taxicab drivers shall always be
   acknowledged.

   1. Social conversational acknowledgment may be accom-
      plished verbally or nonverbally with a smile, nod or other
      polite gestures.

C. Taxicab driver tips shall be determined based upon the overall travel experience. Specifically, the tip shall be calculated
   using four criteria:

   1. The efficiency and speed of the driver
   2. The comfort of the ride
   3. The odor of the taxicab
   4. The odor of the taxicab driver

BOR 13-7 | Passenger Trains

Passenger train travel offers significant advantages over other modes of transportation. First, it is a relaxed and comfortable ride. Passengers may read, work, sleep and eat. And though traveling by rail is often slightly more expensive, it provides a unique view of the country en route from departure to destination. Riding the rails is the safest, most convenient and most pleasurable form of transportation.

A. Train travel is considered recreational and is discouraged for any individual with a specific deadline.

B. Conversation with other passengers is allowable without restriction on trains.

C. Speaking louder than a standard conversational voice is prohibited whenever the train is in motion.

D. The application of graffiti is prohibited on the interior and exterior walls of trains. Graffiti is illegal, hinders the overall travel experience and ultimately results in higher ticket prices.

   1. Individuals choosing to disobey federal law and BOR 13-7 shall honor the Graffiti Applicator's Code: "The application of graffiti shall be done tastefully, professionally and shall contain a socially acceptable message."

   EXAMPLES:

   "My OTHER graffiti is a Mona Lisa"

   "Freedom of speech was guaranteed by our forefathers to ensure that each of us have a voice. I am a fourth-generation American. My great grandfather arrived at Ellis Island in 1892 from Germany. My grandparents and parents struggled

for over a century working nearly 80 hours a week to allow me the freedoms and opportunities I now enjoy. I am a recent graduate of Columbia University specializing in Education. Although currently unemployed, I take great pride in spray painting this message in navy blue shade MB-14 on car number 9 of the Hutchinson, Kansas Express."

BOR 13-8 | Buses

The city bus is an excellent transportation option for the commute or weekend getaway. Riding the bus is inexpensive and eliminates the stress of city parking. Generally operated in urban areas, city buses reduce the number of automobiles on the road.

BOR 13-7. Individuals choosing to disobey federal law and BOR 13-7 shall honor the Graffiti Applicator's Code: "The application of graffiti shall be done tastefully, professionally and shall contain a socially acceptable message."

A. All personal items larger than a purse or laptop computer shall be stored in the overhead bin.

B. Bus drivers shall always be offered a verbal "thank you" prior to exiting.

C. Cell phones are permissible without restriction on all buses except school buses.

D. Investment opportunities disclosed by strangers in bus terminals shall never be seriously considered.

BOR 13-9 | Subways

In an effort to reduce traffic congestion, many large cities have developed mass transit systems including subways, light rail and elevated rail. Mass transit systems transport large numbers of people efficiently in large metropolitan areas. Most systems are owned and operated by local or federal government and are funded and subsidized by tax revenue. Although improvements have been made in recent years, the subway is still a potentially dangerous place. Care should be taken to protect valuables and yourself when riding the subway.

A. Profanity is prohibited on the subway in the presence of children under eighteen.

B. Seats shall be offered to women, the elderly and handicapped or injured individuals when no seats are vacant.

NOTE: If the subway stops suddenly, a standing elderly or injured individual will likely use whatever is readily available to remain balanced.

C. Due to excessive noise and the often unavailability of cell phone service underground, cell phone usage is prohibited on the subway unless an emergency situation exists.

D. The consumption of food is prohibited on the subway.

E. Riding the subway for two stops or less is prohibited, if the distance can be easily walked. This restriction does not apply if:

1. Moderate (or greater) precipitation is occurring (see BOR 4-16 A1a).

2. Any member of a traveling party has a physical restriction.

3. The transport of heavy objects would make walking impractical.

BOR 13-10 | Walking

Whenever practical, walking is the preferred method of transportation. Walking is inexpensive, relieves stress and promotes general health as a low-impact exercise. Many individuals walk as a hobby, and may use a pedometer to track distance and progress. Engaging in a recreational walk is one of the safest forms of exercise and helps ensure mental and physical health.

A. Cell phones are prohibited during recreational walks unless:

1. Cell phone availability is a requirement of employment.
2. A specific incoming call is expected.
3. A unique and nonroutine situation may warrant communication with others.

B. Pedestrians shall always walk facing traffic on roadways without sidewalks.

BOR 13-10. Pedestrians shall always walk facing traffic on roadways without sidewalks.

C. Pedestrians crossing the path of a motor vehicle shall make personal eye contact with the driver prior to initiating passage across the path of a vehicle (see BOR 2-1).

D. Taking a recreational walk with a spouse or significant other provides an excellent opportunity to exercise together. Removing distractions such as television, telephone and children allows couples to communicate effectively, often reducing or eliminating conflict.

E. The right-of-way for pedestrians shall be determined in the following ascending order:

1. Ordinary walkers
2. Men or women pushing a baby stroller
3. Men or women with an obvious physical disability

4. Pregnant women
5. The elderly
6. A pregnant elderly woman with an obvious disability pushing a baby stroller

Hitchhiking

Hitchhiking is the practice of soliciting a ride by extending the fist with the thumb exposed at approaching drivers. The advantages of hitchhiking include flexibility of travel and not worrying about the expense and hassle of a car. The disadvantages include weathering the elements and possible loss of life. "Traveling by finger" is generally discouraged.

BOR 13-11. Hitchhikers shall always offer a tip to the driver. Compensation may be monetary or non-monetary.

A. Hitchhiking should never be attempted at night. As a safe alternative whenever stranded: Don't panic, use a cell phone to call friends or a taxi.

B. Hitchhikers shall always offer a tip to the driver. Compensation may be monetary or non-monetary.

C. As we have learned from the movies, picking up an attractive woman hitchhiking in a swimsuit is extremely dangerous. She is usually accompanied by a carjacker hiding in the bushes waiting to confiscate your car.

BOR 13-12 | Bicycles

Utilizing a bicycle for transportation saves money and serves as an effective low-impact exercise. Numbering over one billion, bicycles currently outnumber automobiles worldwide. Bicycles are utilized in the United States for both transportation and recreation. It is often said that riding a bike is just like riding a bike; you never forget how to do it.

A. All bicycles shall be locked when parked at a public location.

1. Inexpensive combination chain locks are only authorized for bicycles with a value of two hundred dollars or less.

B. Cyclists passing vehicles stuck in traffic are prohibited from making celebratory or belittling expressions or hand gestures at stalled drivers.

C. The following bicycle signals enhance safety and shall be recognized by both motorists and cyclists:

1. Cyclist's left arm is fully extended: The cyclist is preparing to make a left turn.

2. Cyclist's left arm is extended upward: The cyclist is preparing to make a right turn.

3. Cyclist's left arm is extended downward: The cyclist is preparing to slow down or stop.

4. Cyclist is operating a cell phone while in motion: The cyclist is preparing for death. The cyclist is usually in communication with parents or children verifying the accuracy of their last will and testament.

BOR 13-13 | [Intentionally Omitted for Obvious Reasons]

BOR 13-14 | Motorcycles

The motorcycle is the most economic mode of mid- to long-range personal transportation. Motorcycles are typically twice as fuel efficient as automobiles, although higher gas mileage is accompanied with higher risks. Fatal accidents are much more common with motorcycles than automobiles. Helmet wear significantly reduces fatalities in motorcycle accidents and is encouraged.

A. The inherent danger of motorcycle travel mandates the requirement that all riders are reasonably responsible. Reasonable responsibility shall be thoroughly and honestly self-evaluated.

B. Riders may acknowledge other riders on the road by displaying one of the three authorized hand signals:

1. The Low 5: This signal simply acknowledges other drivers.

2. Law Enforcement Caution: This hand signal alerts other bikers of the existence of a nearby police officer.

This gesture is accomplished by pointing in the general direction of the observed position of a law enforcement officer.

3. The Secret Biker's Flash: The method and intent of the secret biker's flash may be disclosed to new riders after one hundred solo riding hours have been completed.

C. Many bikers ride with what they call a "Guardian Bell." This silver bell is attached to a discrete location on the bike. The purpose of the bell is to absorb evil spirits on the road and thereby protect all bikers. Although the protective properties of the bell are highly disputed, it serves as an inexpensive insurance option.

BOR 13-14. Riders may acknowledge other riders on the road by displaying the low 5.

BOR 13-15 | Skateboards

Skateboards are four-wheeled boards designed for both movement and stunts. The skateboard has evolved little since first introduced in the 1970s in California. Most modern skateboards are street boards measuring 30 to 32 inches in length. Since its first appearance in many popular 1980s movies, the skateboard has become increasingly popular among American teenagers. The inherent danger of riding a board with wheels warrants the use of a helmet.

A. The recreational use of skateboards is authorized without restriction for individuals age twenty-three and younger. The use of skateboards is permitted for individuals twenty-four and older only to train or compete in public or professional sporting competitions.

B. Skateboards shall not be given to children under eighteen without verbal consent from a parent or guardian.

EPILOGUE

"You Put the Toilet Paper on Wrong!"

The inspiration for *The Book of Rules* came from an unlikely source. In 1995, I was an active-duty Air Force air traffic controller at Cannon AFB, New Mexico. Air traffic controllers work in the control tower and RADAR approach control facilities at airports (not the personnel on the flight line, who direct the movement of aircraft on the terminal with flashlight type devices—most of America holds this misconception, as I did myself when I enlisted in the Air Force). Shortly before the end of my enlistment, my wife at the time and two kiddos planned our leave to visit my parents in southern Illinois. We arrived, unpacked our bags and began to catch up with family and friends. Later in the evening, I heard my mother yell my full legal name as she walked out of the bathroom. My mother, Janie, is a first-grade school teacher in the St. Louis metropolitan area. I wondered what I had done. Had I broken the antique lamp in the bathroom? Did I accidentally drop a treasured piece of jewelry in the sink? Her exact words, as well as I can recollect were: "Joshua Michael Belter, you put the toilet paper on wrong!" My mother likes the roll of toilet paper to advance with new sheets dispensed from the bottom of the roll. She wasn't really angry—she had a smile on her face after speaking those words. But she was quite serious about her preference to have the toilet paper placed on the roll the "right" way. That really got me thinking. I wondered just how many things in life are not right or wrong, not immoral or illegal, but just the way they are "supposed to be."

That thought stayed with me for over a decade. And it remained a simple thought until my son, Jonathan, and I had an epiphany after viewing a seemingly unimportant event. As we were exiting a department store in Davenport, Iowa, a young mother pushing a baby stroller crossed the lane of traffic in front of the store without first checking for approaching cars. Vehicles in both directions were forced to abruptly stop to prevent a collision. Jonathan looked at me and said, "There should be a rule about walking in front of a vehicle and expecting them to stop." He was so right! There should be a rule! There are hundreds of books about manners and grace, but there is nothing out there about simple common sense.

For several years *The Book of Rules* was nothing more than a collection of ideas. Shoppers really should walk counterclockwise at the mall; pedestrians really should make eye contact with drivers before crossing in front of a car; and most importantly, toilet paper rolls really should be placed with the sheets advancing from the bottom of the roll. This random collection of thoughts and ideas became an inside joke for many of my family and friends. New ideas were often suggested to be included in the rule book.

In the spring of 2007, I wondered if I had enough information to write a book. I began by casually interviewing friends and co-workers. What are your pet peeves? What really bothers you when you are out in public? What did Miss Manners forget to write in her book of manners? I finally had enough information to start the project.

About This Book

The first publication of *The Book of Rules* was released as *The Book of Rules 94.7A, The Definitive Guide to Living Life*. Most formal workplace manuals have a number in the title, and the number 94.7 was a tribute to my favorite radio station in St. Louis, Missouri, K-SHE 95.

Every regulation in *The Book of Rules* was reviewed by several hundred co-workers, friends, relatives and strangers who never quite understood why I valued their opinion about "wearing socks with sandals" or "using a cell phone in the car." Although each regulation in *The Book of Rules* is debatable, I generally went with the consensus when determining the direction for each rule in the handbook. One notable exception is BOR 8-1 C, Toilet Paper Placement. It is worth mentioning that a little over half of the individuals interviewed for this book indicated their preference to place toilet paper rolls with new sheets advancing from the top of the roll. But I had to stay true to my mother, Janie, the inspiration for this book.

The Book of Rules Regulatory Board is a real organization. The board is comprised of family and friends who were instrumental in the development of the project. We truly encourage each and every reader to be an active part of *The Book of Rules*. ALL submissions from readers that suggest additions and amendments are considered by The Book of Rules Regulatory Board for each successive update.

Special thanks to Andy Mason and Anne Jezek for your ideas, inspiration and extensive editing. Andy Mason's idea for Appendix C was added at the eleventh hour. Thank you to Jonathan Belter and Jacob Albert for your creative ideas for the critical first four chapters of the book. Thanks to Jason Koonce, Heidi Vascek and Jim Snow for your wonderful individual suggestions. And thank you to Jenna Belter for your help in the initial promotion and marketing of the project.

It's amazing how a simple comment like my mother chastising my toilet paper placement can change the direction, goals and aspirations of several lives simultaneously.

Music is one of the most important things in my life. I sing all of the harmony vocals for the group Fast Time Constant. My musical idol, John Lennon, said in 1980 (shortly before his death), "Life is what happens while you're busy making other plans."

SPECIAL THANKS TO THE

BOOK OF RULES REGULATORY BOARD

Jonathan Belter

Jenna Belter

Andy Mason

Anne Jezek

Jacob Albert

About the Author

Joshua Belter is an air traffic controller and singer for the band Fast Time Constant. He was inspired to create *The Book of Rules* after a toilet-paper incident while visiting his mother's home. For more information, visit www.thebookofrules.com.

APPENDIX A

BOR D-1

DISCREPANCY FORM

(BOR 1-5) All American adults have a primary responsibility to issue BOR D-1 discrepancy forms to individuals when violations to the BOR are personally observed. No other action is warranted or required. The violator alone has the specific requirement to ensure that corrective measures will be taken to become compliant with the BOR.

Violator Name:

Issued By:

Location of Violation:

Date and Time of Violation:

BOR Regulation Violated:

Violator Personally Notified: (Y/N)

Briefly Describe Violation:

APPENDIX B

BOR S-1

SUBMISSION FORM

BOR S-1 **SUBMISSION FORM** *Previous versions are obsolete* **(see BOR 1-7)**	**THE BOOK OF RULES** *Promoting Excellence* *in America Since 2008* **www.thebookofrules.com**

(BOR 1-7) Unsolicited submissions regarding amendments and additions to the BOR are encouraged. Submissions may be proposed in writing by completing this form or by following the instructions online at www.thebookofrules.com. Submissions become the property of the BOR Regulatory Board after receipt and will not be returned. The inclusion decision will be determined solely by the BOR Regulatory Board.

Name:

Address:

City:

State: Zip:

E-mail:

SUBMISSIONS MAY BE MAILED TO:
The Book of Rules Regulatory Board, P.O. Box 2413, Keller, TX 76244

APPENDIX C

BOR G-1

UTILITY FORM

INDEX

CHECK OUT ANOTHER GREAT BOOK FROM HOW!

The Art of Manliness

While it's definitely more than just monster trucks, grilling and six-pack abs, true manliness is hard to define. Taking lessons from classic gentlemen such as Benjamin Franklin and Theodore Roosevelt, authors Brett and Kate McKay have created a collection of the most useful advice every man needs to know. This book contains a wealth of information that ranges from survival skills to social skills to advice on how to improve your character. Whether you are braving the wilds with your friends, courting your girlfriend or raising a family, you'll gain practical information and inspiration for every area of life.

**FIND THIS BOOK AND MANY OTHERS
AT MYDESIGNSHOP.COM OR YOUR LOCAL BOOKSTORE**

SPECIAL OFFER FROM HOW BOOKS!

You can get 15% off your entire order at MyDesignShop.com! All you have to do is go to www.howdesign.com/howbooks-offer and sign up for our free e-newsletter on graphic design. You'll also get a free digital download of the latest issue of *HOW* magazine.

 For behind-the-scenes information and special offers, become a fan of our Facebook page: **facebook.com/HOWbooks**

 For more news, tips and articles, follow us on Twitter: **@HOWbrand**